SCHOLASTIC

GET READY FOR 2ND GRADE

Cover design by Josue Castilleja; Cover art by Bernard Adnet

ISBN 0-439-60626-8
Copyright © 2004 by Scholastic Inc. All rights reserved. Printed in the U.S.A.

4 5 6 7 8 9 10   40   09 08 07 06

New York • Toronto • London • Auckland • Sydney
Mexico City • New Delhi • Hong Kong • Buenos Aires

Teaching *Resources*

Table of Contents

Dear Parent:

Congratulations! You hold in your hands an exceptional educational tool that will give your child a head start into the coming school year.

Inside this book, you'll find one hundred practice pages that will help your child review and learn reading and writing skills, grammar, addition and subtraction, and so much more! *Get Ready for 2nd Grade* is divided into 10 weeks, with two practice pages for each day of the week, Monday to Friday. However, feel free to use the pages in any order that your child would like. Here are other features you'll find inside:

- A weekly **incentive chart** to motivate and reward your child for his or her efforts.

- A sheet of **colorful stickers** to add to the incentive chart. There are small stickers for completing the activities each day, as well as a large sticker to use as a weekly reward.

- Suggestions for fun, creative **learning activities** you can do with your child each week.

- A **recommended reading list** of age-appropriate books that you and your child can read throughout the summer.

- A **super-fun, full-color game board** that folds out from the back of the book. You'll also find a sheet of game cards and playing pieces.

- A **certificate of completion** to celebrate your child's accomplishments.

We hope you and your child will have a lot of fun as you work together to complete this workbook.

Enjoy!
The editors

Terrific Tips for Using This Book

1 Pick a good time for your child to work on the activities. You may want to do it around mid-morning after play, or early afternoon when your child is not too tired.

2 Make sure your child has all the supplies he or she needs, such as pencils and crayons. Set aside a special place for your child to work.

3 At the beginning of each week, discuss with your child how many minutes a day he or she would like to read. Write the goal at the top of the incentive chart for the week. (We recommend reading 15 to 20 minutes a day with your child who is entering 2nd grade.)

4 Reward your child's efforts with the small stickers at the end of each day. As an added bonus, let your child affix a large sticker at the bottom of the incentive chart for completing the activities each week.

5 Encourage your child to complete the worksheet, but don't force the issue. While you may want to ensure that your child succeeds, it's also important that your child maintain a positive and relaxed attitude toward school and learning.

6 For more summertime fun, invite your child to play the colorful, skills-based game board at the back of the book. Your child can play the game with you or with friends and siblings.

7 When your child has finished the workbook, present him or her with the certificate of completion at the back of the book. Feel free to frame or laminate the certificate and display it on the wall for everyone to see. Your child will be so proud!

Helping Your Child Get Ready: Week 1

These are the skills your child will be working on this week.

Math
- adding and subtracting through 10
- odd and even numbers

Reading
- finding the main idea
- reading for details

Vocabulary
- examining similarities
- -ank word family

Grammar
- capitalization
- word order

Handwriting
- uppercase and lowercase manuscript letters

Here are some activities you and your child might enjoy.

Summer's Here! While looking at a calendar with your child, encourage him or her to find the first day of summer. Then ask questions such as *How many days until the next full moon? How many weeks until autumn? How many months until your birthday?*

My Summer Plan Suggest that your child come up with a plan to achieve a goal by the end of the summer. Help him or her map out a way to be successful. Periodically, check to see how he or she is progressing.

How Hot Is It? Play a guessing game. Ask your child to estimate the temperature outdoors. Then, help your child find out what the actual temperature is. Ask: *Is it warmer or cooler indoors? By how much?*

Sun Safety Talk about sun safety with your child. Ask him or her to draw a picture that shows how to stay safe in the sun.

Your child might enjoy reading the following books.

Flat Stanley
by Jeff Brown

Amelia Bedelia
by Peggy Parish

Tar Beach
by Faith Ringgold

_____ 's Incentive Chart: Week 1

Name Here

This week, I plan to read_____ minutes each day.

CHART YOUR PROGRESS HERE.

Week 1	Day 1	Day 2	Day 3	Day 4	Day 5
I read for...	minutes	minutes	minutes	minutes	minutes
Put a sticker to show you completed each day's work.					

Congratulations!

Wow! You did a great job this week!

#1

Place sticker here.

Parent or Caregiver's Signature _____

A–Z

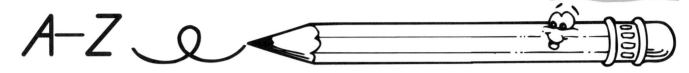

Trace and write the alphabet.

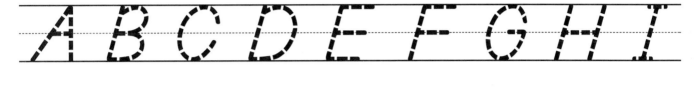

A B C D E F G H I

J K L M N O P Q R

S T U V W X Y Z

Capitalizing Names

Sometimes the names of people, places, and things are special. They begin with a **capital letter**.

Circle the special names in the picture. Write each one correctly on a line.

1. _____

2. _____

3. _____

4. _____

a–z

Trace and write the alphabet.

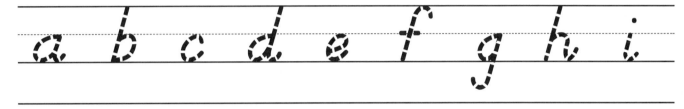

a b c d e f g h i

j k l m n o p q r

s t u v w x y z

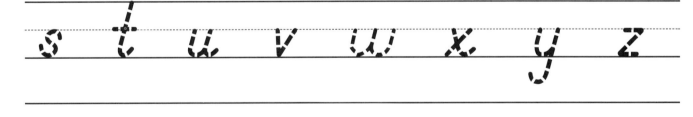

abcd

Grouping Things

Sort the things listed below into groups. Write each word from the list in the correct box.

doll

yellow

ball

apple

bread

green

game

red

pasta

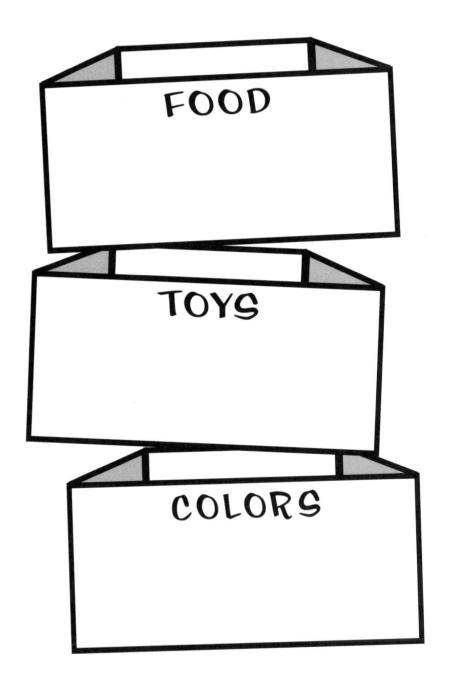

FOOD

TOYS

COLORS

Look at the things in each group. How does each thing fit into the group?

Scholastic Teaching Resources   *Get Ready for 2nd Grade*

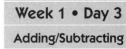
Shapes on a Snake

Add or subtract.

A. ♡6 + ④ = 10

B. ▢ − ◇ = ____

C. ◯ − ⬡ = ____

D. ◯ + ♡ = ____

E. ▭ + ⬡ = ____

F. ⬡ + ⬡ = ____

G. ◇ + ⬡ = ____

H. ♡ + ◯ = ____

I. △ − ▭ = ____

J. ▢ − ⬡ = ____

Scholastic Teaching Resources   Get Ready for 2nd Grade

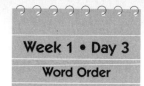

Mixed-Up Words

Words in a sentence must be in an order that makes sense.

These words are mixed up. Put them in order. Then write each sentence.

1. snow. bear likes This

_____

2. water cold. The is

_____

3. fast. The runs bear

_____

4. play. bears Two

_____

Scholastic Teaching Resources   *Get Ready for 2nd Grade*

Trucks

 The **main idea** *tells what the whole story is about.*

   Trucks do important work. Dump trucks carry away sand and rocks. Cement trucks have a barrel that turns around and around. They deliver cement to workers who are making sidewalks. Fire trucks carry water hoses and firefighters. Gasoline is delivered in large tank trucks. Flatbed trucks carry wood to the people who are building houses.

Find the sentence in the story that tells the main idea. Write it in the circle below. Then draw a line from the main idea to all the trucks that were described in the story.

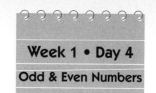

Patterns for the Mail Carrier

Meimei the mail carrier is delivering letters. Give her some help. Fill in the missing addresses on the houses below.

Extra

What pattern do you see in the house numbers? _____

_____

_____

_____

Scholastic Teaching Resources   Get Ready for 2nd Grade

Going to Grammy's

Kelly is going to spend the night with her grandmother. She will need to take her pajamas, a shirt, and some shorts. Into the suitcase go her toothbrush, toothpaste, and hairbrush. Grammy told her to bring a swimsuit in case it was warm enough to swim. Mom said to pack her favorite pillow and storybooks. Dad said, "Don't forget to take Grammy's sunglasses that she left here last week." Now Kelly is ready to go!

1. Color the things that Kelly packed in her suitcase.

2. A **compound word** is a big word that is made up of two little words. For example, cow + boy = cowboy. Find 8 compound words in this story and circle them.

  On a separate sheet of paper, make a list of things you would pack if you were going to spend the night at your grandmother's house.

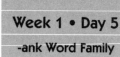
-ank Words

Unscramble each word. Write it on the line.

nkpla _____

ankb _____

ktan _____

canrk _____

ankdr _____

ktans _____

bklan _____

nkya _____

Find and circle each word from the Word Bank.

```
p r m b i n a t a n k i o h r s t a n k
c k l b n k d r a n k r n a r t y j h j
i l r b l a n k r i o n a c r a n k e w
k a y a n k i b k r c a r n k y u r k n
n k r n a f l a n k i c y x r p l a n k
u r k n a k b a n k r n i s a n k v a k
```

Word Bank

bank   plank

blank   sank

crank   stank

drank   tank

flank   yank

Write a sentence using one of the -ank family words.

_____

_____

Scholastic Teaching Resources   Get Ready for 2nd Grade

Helping Your Child Get Ready: Week 2

These are the skills your child will be working on this week.

Math
- adding and subtracting through 10
- problem solving
- adding double numbers to 18

Reading
- real or fantasy
- sequencing

Writing
- adjectives
- writing to a prompt

Vocabulary
- initial and final consonants
- -ash word family

Grammar
- sentence subjects and predicates

Here are some activities you and your child might enjoy.

Rainbow Hunt Ask your child to find one object for each color of the rainbow: red, orange, yellow, green, blue, and purple.

Scrambled Names Have your child write his or her first and last name on a sheet of paper and cut apart the letters. Encourage your child to use the letters to make new words. For variety, your child might also use the names of friends and family members.

Daily Time Line Help your child practice sequencing by creating a time line of the daily routine. Encourage him or her to draw pictures or write words to describe what happened first, next, and so on.

Find Your Way Home Invite your child to make a map of the place you live. He or she can draw and label what is in front, behind, to the left, and to the right of your home.

Your child might enjoy reading the following books.

The Great Kapok Tree
by Lynne Cherry

Chato's Kitchen
by Gary Soto

The Velveteen Rabbit
by Margery Williams

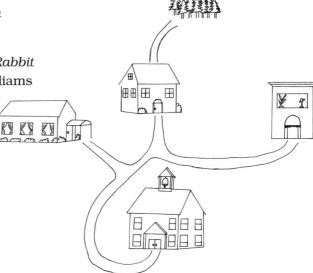

_____'s Incentive Chart: Week 2

This week, I plan to read _____ minutes each day.

CHART YOUR PROGRESS HERE.

Week 2 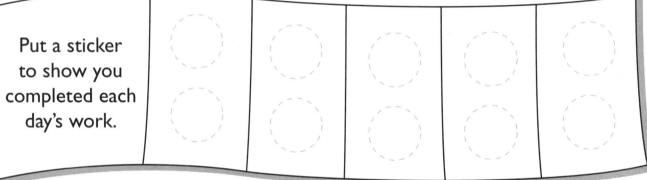 I read for...	Day 1	Day 2	Day 3	Day 4	Day 5
	minutes	minutes	minutes	minutes	minutes
Put a sticker to show you completed each day's work.					

Congratulations!

Wow! You did a great job this week!

#1

Place sticker here.

Parent or Caregiver's Signature _____

Down the Word Steps

Work your way down the word steps.

The last letter of each word is the first letter of a new word.

Use the picture clues to help you.

Sensational Words

Choose words from the Word Bank to describe each picture.

It tastes _____.

It looks _____.

It feels _____.

Word Bank

bumpy

crunchy

furry

gray

red

salty

smooth

squeaky

sweet

It feels _____.

It tastes _____.

It sounds _____.

It looks _____.

It sounds _____.

It feels _____.

Find two objects outside. On another piece of paper, write two adjectives to describe each object.

Scholastic Teaching Resources *Get Ready for 2nd Grade*

Mr. Lee's Store

*Story events that can really happen are **real**. Story events that are make-believe are **fantasy**.*

At night, Mr. Lee locked the store and went home. That's when the fun began! The ketchup bottles stood in rows like bowling pins. Then the watermelon rolled down the aisle and knocked them down. The chicken wings flew around the room. Cans of soup stacked themselves higher and higher until they laughed so hard that they tumbled over. Carrots danced with bananas. Then it was morning. "Get back in your places!" called the milk jug. "Mr. Lee is coming!" Mr. Lee opened the door and went right to work.

Circle the cans that are make-believe.

ketchup bottles and a watermelon bowling

a talking milk jug

dancing bananas

chicken wings that can fly all by themselves

Mr. Lee went to work.

laughing soup cans

Mr. Lee went home at night.

dancing carrots

a grocery store

Draw a picture of the story on another piece of paper.

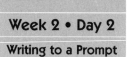
In Warm Weather

 When it is warm outside, what do you like to do?
Draw a picture to show something you like to do.

When it is warm outside, I like to _____

_____

I like doing this because _____

_____

When it is warm, I like to go to _____

_____

I like warm weather because _____

_____

Planes . . . Trains . . .

Add or subtract.

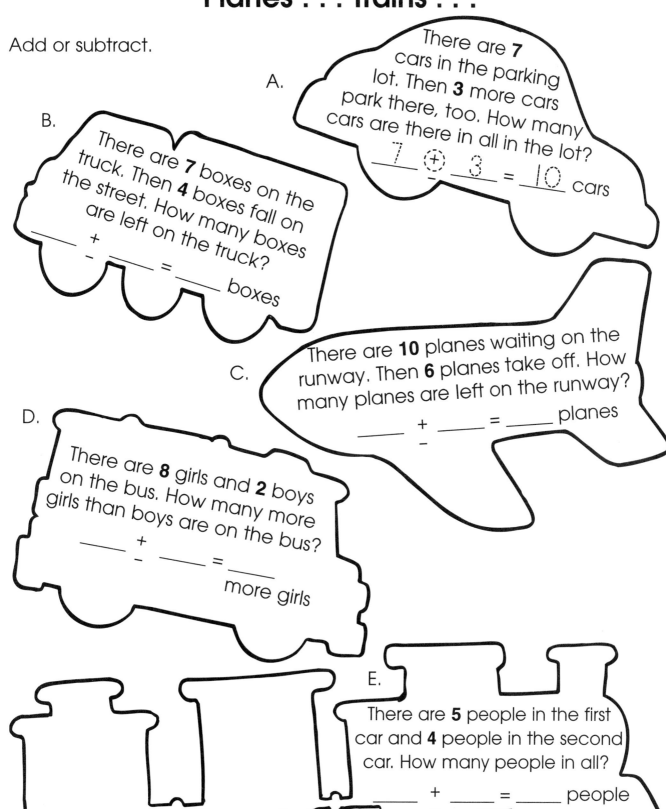

A. There are **7** cars in the parking lot. Then **3** more cars park there, too. How many cars are there in all in the lot?

7 (+) 3 = 10 cars

B. There are **7** boxes on the truck. Then **4** boxes fall on the street. How many boxes are left on the truck?

_____ + _____ = _____ boxes

C. There are **10** planes waiting on the runway. Then **6** planes take off. How many planes are left on the runway?

_____ + _____ = _____ planes

D. There are **8** girls and **2** boys on the bus. How many more girls than boys are on the bus?

_____ + _____ = _____ more girls

E. There are **5** people in the first car and **4** people in the second car. How many people in all?

_____ + _____ = _____ people

-ash Words

Unscramble each word. Write it on the line.

sthra _____   asmh _____

flhas _____   rhas _____

scha _____   hapssl _____

ssah _____   hcsra _____

Find and circle each word from the Word Bank.

s p x f h f r a s h x s n a g p p s h f

p s h f s n p s h f s p l a s h p s h f

c r a s h f s h n a g p p s h f c a s h

d p s r h w s a s h i r c m a s h i b v

s t a s h f g i s n a p t r a s h d s f

f g p f l a s h s n i a s m a s h b j k

Word Bank

cash sash

crash smash

flash splash

mash stash

rash trash

Write a sentence using one of the –ash family words.

_____

_____

_____

_____

24

Who Does It?

The **subject** of a sentence tells who or what did something.

Read the sentences below. Look at the picture to find out who or what is doing the action described in the sentence and then write it on the line.

1. A _____ sits in the wagon.

2. A _____ rides in the wagon too.

3. _____ is pulling the wagon.

4. Her _____ wants a ride too.

5. The _____ can carry all the animals.

6. The _____ fly along with them.

Write another sentence about the picture. Underline the subject of the sentence.

_____

What Happens?

The **predicate** of a sentence tells what happens.

For each sentence, write an ending that tells what is happening in the picture.

1. The cat _____ .

2. A mouse _____ .

3. The cat _____ .

4. The mouse _____ .

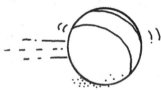

5. The ball _____ .

6. The water _____ .

Write another sentence about the cat and mouse. Underline the part of the sentence that tells what happens.

_____

Scholastic Teaching Resources   Get Ready for 2nd Grade

Swimming Lessons

 Sequencing *means putting the events in a story in the order they happened.*

Last summer I learned how to swim. First, the teacher told me to hold my breath. Then I learned to put my head under water. I practiced kicking my feet. While I held on to a float, I paddled around the pool. Next, I floated to my teacher with my arms straight out. Finally, I swam using both my arms and my legs. I did it! Swimming is fun! This summer, I want to learn to dive off the diving board.

Number the pictures in the order that they happened in the story.

Unscramble the letters to tell what the person in the story wants to do next.

EALNR   **OT**   **IVDE**

____ ____ ____ ____ ____   ____ ____   ____ ____ ____ ____

Not Far From Home

Start at  Write the number of steps. Add.

steps to + steps home = _____ steps   steps to + steps home = _____ steps

_7_ + _7_ = _14_

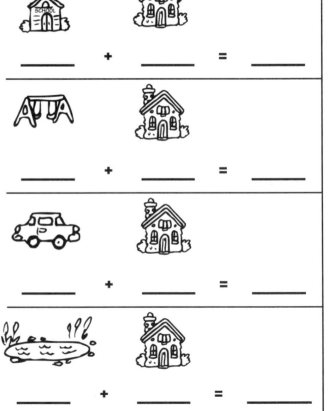

Scholastic Teaching Resources   *Get Ready for 2nd Grade*

Helping Your Child Get Ready: Week 3

These are the skills your child will be working on this week.

Math
- identifying patterns
- writing equations

Reading
- following directions
- drawing conclusions

Writing
- writing to a prompt
- writing statements

Vocabulary
- short vowels
- -ick word family

Grammar
- capitalization

Here are some activities you and your child might enjoy.

Silly Summer Sentences How can *summer* turn into a tongue twister? Guide your child to make up a sentence using the word summer and as many other words as possible that start with *s*.

What's Your Estimate? Ask your child to estimate how many times in 60 seconds he or she can . . .

a) say "Mississippi"   **b)** write his or her name

Then have him or her try each activity and compare the results with the estimate.

Words Can Add Up Assign a monetary value to words. For example, a consonant can be worth one penny and a vowel can be worth one nickel. Challenge your child to find a word with a high value.

Room With a View Invite your child to look out of a window. Have your child describe or draw ten things in the scene. Remind your child to use lots of detail.

Your child might enjoy reading the following books.

Why Mosquitoes Buzz in People's Ears
by Verna Aardema

Fathers, Mothers, Sisters, Brothers
by Mary Ann Hoberman

Thank You, Mr. Falker
by Patricia Polacco

_____ **'s Incentive Chart: Week 3**
Name Here

This week, I plan to read _____ minutes each day.

CHART YOUR PROGRESS HERE.

Week 3	Day 1	Day 2	Day 3	Day 4	Day 5
I read for...	minutes	minutes	minutes	minutes	minutes
Put a sticker to show you completed each day's work.					

Congratulations!

Wow! You did a great job this week!

Parent or Caregiver's Signature _____

Place sticker here.

Short Vowel Tic Tac

Say the picture names.

Find and color 3 pictures in a row with the same short vowel sound.

1. Short-*a* sound as in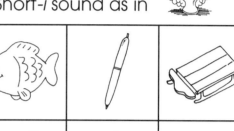

2. Short-*i* sound as in

3. Short-*e* sound as in

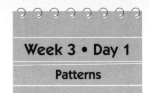
Pattern Learner

A **pattern** is a repeated arrangement of numbers, shapes, or lines in a row.
Continue the patterns below.

1. 324, 435, 546,

2. [pattern of shapes: square, circle, triangle, square, circle]

3. [pattern of bracket shapes]

4. [pattern of squares with lines]

5. [pattern of stick figures]

6. [pattern of flowers]

7. A C E G I K

8. 11:05, 11:10, 11:15,

9. [pattern: sun, star, moon, sun]

Scholastic Teaching Resources   Get Ready for 2nd Grade

Polly Want a Cracker?

Hello.

Hello, hello.

Have you ever heard a parrot talk? Parrots are able to copy sounds that they hear. You can train a parrot to repeat words, songs, and whistles. But a parrot cannot say words that it has never heard. People can use words to make new sentences, but a parrot cannot.

Read each sentence. If it is true, color the parrot under True. If it is false, color the parrot under False.

True   False

1. You could teach a parrot to sing "Happy Birthday."

2. You could ask a parrot any question, and it could give the answer.

3. A parrot could make up a fairy tale.

4. If a parrot heard your mom say, "Brush your teeth," every night, he could learn to say it, too.

5. It is possible for a parrot to repeat words in Spanish.

Write what would happen if a parrot heard you say, "No, I can't" too often.

33

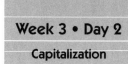

Title Words

Important words in a title are capitalized.

Circle all the words that are capitalized.

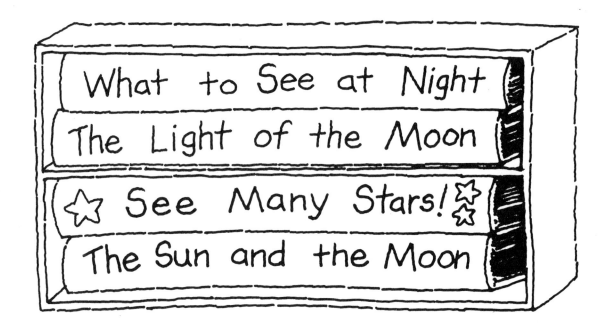

What to See at Night

The Light of the Moon

☆ See Many Stars! ☆

The Sun and the Moon

Now use some of the words from the titles above to write your own titles.

_____

_____

_____

_____

Scholastic Teaching Resources   Get Ready for 2nd Grade

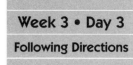

Fun at the Beach

Jack and Joni went to the beach today. Mom spread a blanket on the sand, and they had a picnic. It got very hot, so Jack and Joni jumped into the cold water. They climbed onto a big yellow raft. The waves made the raft go up and down. Later, they played in the sand and built sandcastles. Jack and Joni picked up pretty shells. Joni found a starfish. What a fun day!

1. Color the pictures below that are from the story. Put an X on the ones that don't belong.

2. In the third sentence, find two words that are opposites of each other and circle them with a red crayon.

3. In the fifth sentence, find two more words that are opposites of each other and circle them with a blue crayon.

4. Draw a box around the compound word that tells what Joni found.

5. What color was the raft? Show your answer by coloring the picture at the top of the page.

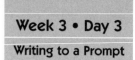

All About Our Flag

 Add stars and stripes to the flag below and color them in.

The colors of the American flag are _____

The American flag has _____

These are places where I see the American flag: _____

_____

People display the American flag because _____

_____

Scholastic Teaching Resources   Get Ready for 2nd Grade

More Title Words

Important words in a title are capitalized.

Read the titles. Circle all the words that should be capitalized.

1. look at the stars!

2. the moon shines at night

3. we see planets

4. many moons shine

5. night and day

Read each set of titles. Draw a line under the correct title.

6. The Sun in the Sky

    the sun in the sky

7. See the stars!

    See the Stars!

-ick Words

Unscramble each word. Write it on the line.

skic _____   kicl _____

ckik _____   icslk _____

kchic _____   tkhic _____

cpik _____   ktric _____

Find and circle each word from the Word Bank.

e u y c k v c h b l k i c k t h c e k f

b j k t r i c k s p x f h q u i c k c k

u y v b l w i c k u y v b l c h i c k w

c k p i c k s p c h c k x f h s l i c k

t f h l i c k u c h y v b c k l s i c k

s p c c k h x f h t h i c k b c k j k h

Word Bank

chick   sick

kick   slick

lick   thick

pick   trick

quick   wick

Write a sentence using one of the –ick family words.

_____

_____

_____

_____

38

Coin-Toss Addition

Toss 6 coins. Write **H** for heads or **T** for tails in the circles below to show your toss. Then write the addition equation. Write the number of "heads" first. We did the first one for you. Try it five times.

(H)(H)(H)(H)(T)(T) Equation: __4 + 2 = 6__

◯◯◯◯◯◯ Equation: _____

◯◯◯◯◯◯ Equation: _____

◯◯◯◯◯◯ Equation: _____

◯◯◯◯◯◯ Equation: _____

◯◯◯◯◯◯ Equation: _____

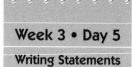
That Sounds Fishy to Me

 A **telling sentence** *begins with a* **capital letter** *and ends with a* **period**.

Write a sentence about each fish. Remember to tell a complete idea.

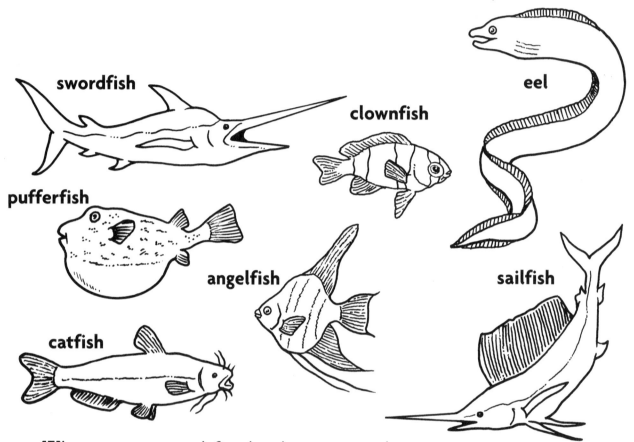

swordfish

clownfish

eel

pufferfish

angelfish

sailfish

catfish

1. The swordfish has a long snout

2. _____

3. _____

4. _____

5. _____

6. _____

7. _____

40

Helping Your Child Get Ready: Week 4

These are the skills your child will be working on this week.

Math
- adding and subtracting through 18
- adding and subtracting with three addends

Reading
- visualizing
- making inferences

Writing
- punctuating questions

Vocabulary
- final consonants
- -ight word family

Grammar
- sentence types: telling, questions, exclamations, command

Here are some activities you and your child might enjoy.

Starring Role All children like to hear stories about themselves. Help your child feel like a star by sharing memories of your child, finding stories with characters that have your child's name, or when reading aloud to your child, insert his or her name in place of the main character's.

Compound Interest Point out examples of compound words to your child. Then have him or her keep track of the compound words heard during an hour. Try it another time and challenge your child to improve on his or her last "score."

The Case of the Mysterious Sock Invite your child to find a secret object to put in a sock. Try to guess what it is by feeling the object through the sock. Trade places. Play again.

Start Collecting Having a collection is a great way for a child to develop higher-level thinking skills like sorting and analyzing. Encourage your child to start one. Leaves, rocks, stamps, or shells are all easy and fun things to collect.

Your child might enjoy reading the following books.

Everybody Cooks Rice
by Norah Dooley

Chester's Way
by Kevin Henkes

Stuart Little
by E.B. White

_____ 's Incentive Chart: Week 4

Name Here

This week, I plan to read _____ minutes each day.

CHART YOUR PROGRESS HERE.

Week 4  I read for...	Day 1	Day 2	Day 3	Day 4	Day 5
	minutes	minutes	minutes	minutes	minutes
Put a sticker to show you completed each day's work.	◯ ◯	◯ ◯	◯ ◯	◯ ◯	◯ ◯

Congratulations!

Wow! You did a great job this week!

#1

Place sticker here.

Parent or Caregiver's Signature _____

Race Through the Facts

Add or subtract. The race car that ends with the highest number wins the race!

$7 + 2 =$ ___ $- 4 =$ ___ $- 3 =$ ___ $+ 9 =$ ___ $+ 5 =$ ___ $- 8 =$ ___ $+ 4 =$ ___ $- 9 =$ ___ $+ 7 =$ ___ $- 6 =$ ___ $+ 3 =$ ___ $- 2 =$ ___ $+ 7 =$ ___ $+ 1 =$ ___ $- 8 =$ ___ $- 11 =$ ___ $- 5 =$ ___ $+ 2 =$ ___ $+ 3 =$ ___ $- 3 =$ ___

$12 - 3 =$ ___ $- 6 =$ ___ $+ 2 =$ ___ $+ 9 =$ ___ $+ 4 =$ ___ $+ 9 =$ ___ $- 9 =$ ___ $+ 6 =$ ___ $+ 1 =$ ___ $- 9 =$ ___ $+ 4 =$ ___ $+ 13 =$ ___ $- 7 =$ ___ $+ 3 =$ ___

Color the winning race car blue.

Ask Mother Goose

 *A sentence that asks a question ends with a **question mark** (?).*
It often begins with one of these words.

Who . . .	*Where . . .*	*Why . . .*	*Could . . .*
What . . .	*When . . .*	*Will . . .*	

Rewrite the questions using capital letters and
question marks.

1. where is the king's castle

   _____

2. who helped Humpty Dumpty

   _____

3. why did the cow jump over the moon

   _____

4. will the frog become a prince

   _____

5. could the three mice see

   _____

Scholastic Teaching Resources   *Get Ready for 2nd Grade*

A Stormy Day

Big, black clouds appeared in the sky. Lightning struck the tallest tree. The scared cow cried, "Moo!" It rained hard. Soon there was a mud puddle by the barn door. Hay blew out of the barn window.

Read the story above. Then go back and read each sentence again. Add to the picture everything that the sentences describe.

Telling Sentences and Questions

A **telling sentence** tells something. It begins with a capital letter and ends with a period.

A **question** asks something. It begins with a capital letter and ends with a question mark.

Underline the capital letter that begins each sentence. Add a period (.) if it is a telling sentence. Add a question mark (?) if it is a question.

1. The vet is nice _____

2. She helped my dog _____

3. Did she see your cat _____

4. Is the cat well now _____

5. My cat feels better _____

The order of the words in a sentence can change its meaning. Change the word order in the telling sentence to make it a question. Write the question.

6. He will take the cat home.

_____

Scholastic Teaching Resources   *Get Ready for 2nd Grade*

What Do You See?

Say the words.

Listen for the ending sounds.

Use the Ending Sounds Color Code to make a picture.

Ending Sounds Color Code				
blue = s	green = t	black = d	red = l	white = m

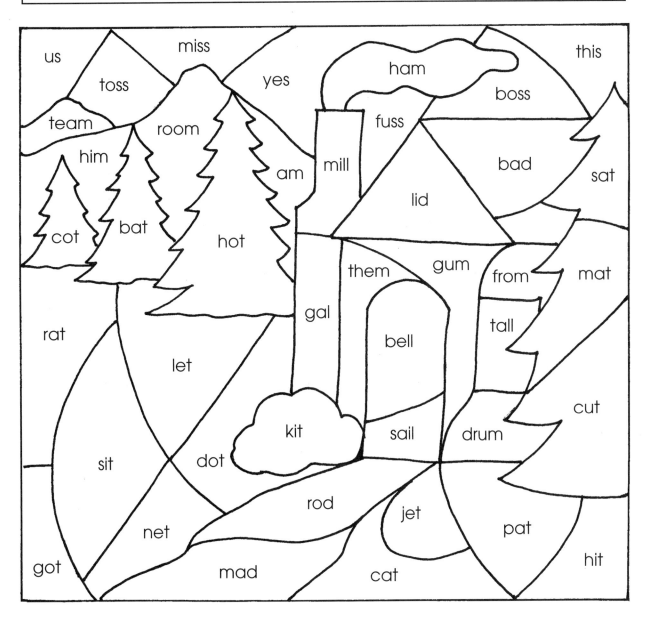

Exclamations and Commands

An **exclamation** shows strong feelings, such as excitement, surprise, or fear. It begins with a capital letter and ends with an exclamation mark (!).

A **command** makes a request or tells someone to do something. It ends with a period or an exclamation mark.

Read each sentence. Write E if the sentence is an exclamation. Write C if the sentence is a command.

1. Ruby copies Angela! _____

2. Look at their dresses. _____

3. They're exactly the same! _____

4. Angela is mad! _____

5. Look at Ruby! _____

6. Show Angela how Ruby hops. _____

Write each sentence correctly.

Exclamation be yourself

7. _____

Command don't copy other people

8. _____

Scholastic Teaching Resources   *Get Ready for 2nd Grade*

A Perfect Strike

Fill in the missing number.

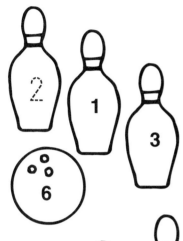

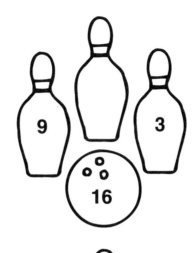

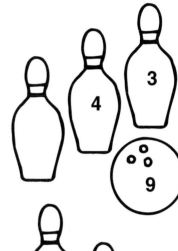

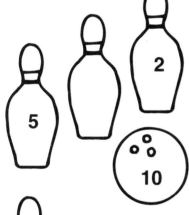

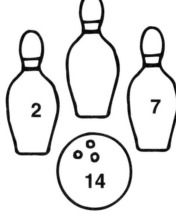

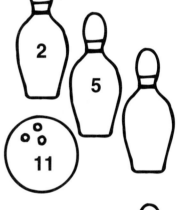

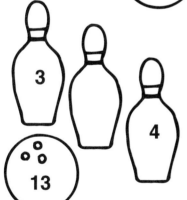

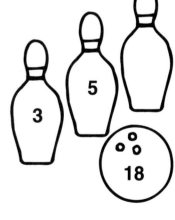

Find three different ways to make 8 with 3 numbers.

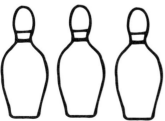

Types of Sentences; Capital I

A **telling sentence** begins with a capital letter and ends with a period.

A **question** begins with a capital letter and ends with a question mark.

An **exclamation** begins with a capital letter and ends with an exclamation mark.

A **command** begins with a capital letter and ends with a period. The word **I** is always capitalized in a sentence.

Decide if each sentence is a telling sentence, a question, an exclamation, or a command. Write T, Q, E, or C on the lines.

1. My sister and I went to the lake. _____

2. Come see this. _____

3. I saw three little sailboats. _____

4. Put the boat in the water. _____

5. Did I have a good time? _____

6. You bet! I loved it! _____

7. Can I go again soon? _____

What would you do at the lake? Use the word **I** and your own ideas to finish the sentences.

8. At the lake _____ saw _____ .

9. _____ can _____ .

10. My friend and _____ liked _____ best.

Scholastic Teaching Resources   *Get Ready for 2nd Grade*

Who Am I?

 Use details from the story to make decisions about the characters.

Circle the picture that answers the riddle.

1. I have feathers. I also have wings, but I don't fly. I love to swim in icy water. Who am I?

2. I am 3 weeks old. I drink milk. I cry when my diaper is wet. Who am I?

3. I live in the ocean. I swim around slowly, looking for something to eat. I have six more arms than you have. Who am I?

4. I am an insect. If you touch me, I might bite you! I make tunnels under the ground. I love to come to your picnic! Who am I?

5. I am a female. I like to watch movies and listen to music. My grandchildren love my oatmeal cookies. Who am I?

6. I am a large mammal. I live in the woods. I have fur. I stand up and growl when I am angry. Who am I?

7. I wear a uniform. My job is to help people. I ride on a big red truck. Who am I?

-ight Words

Unscramble each word. Write it on the line.

htgfli _____   fgriht _____

igtknh _____   htmig _____

htfig _____   thlig _____

slhigt _____   httig _____

Find and circle each word from the Word Bank.

f l i g h t s p c b j k h m i g h t f h

t s i h i d f d e b j s p h s d e t r i

u y b l s i g h t t h f k n i g h t h g

f i g h t s p c b j k h x f h t i g h t

t h f r i g h t u y v b c l i g h t h t

c s l i g h t h v h f s r i g h t u t y

Word Bank

fight   might

flight   right

fright   sight

knight   slight

light   tight

Write a sentence using one of the –ight family words.

_____

_____

_____

Scholastic Teaching Resources   Get Ready for 2nd Grade

Helping Your Child Get Ready: Week 5

These are the skills your child will be working on this week.

Math
- adding and subtracting 2-digit numbers
- coin identity and value

Reading
- compare/contrast
- comprehension

Vocabulary
- sight words
- -ill word family

Grammar
- sentence types: statements, questions
- common nouns

Handwriting
- manuscript numbers 1–10

Here are some activities you and your child might enjoy.

Word Chain Develop your child's listening skills by playing Word Chain. In this game, someone says a word, and the next person must say a word that begins with the last letter of the previous player's word.

Connecting Words Give your child a word and encourage him or her to tell you the thing that often goes with it, such as peanut butter (and jelly) or thunder (and lightning). Or, make analogy pairs such as finger and hand (and toe and foot). Playing word association games can help your child build vocabulary by making connections between words.

Fruit Kebobs Your child can practice patterning by creating a tasty snack. Using a small wooden skewer and a selection of three different fruits, such as grapes, strawberries, and banana slices, invite your child to create a pattern with the fruit. Encourage your child to describe the pattern to you, or suggest a pattern for your child to use such as ABCABC or ABACABAC.

Now You See It, Now You Don't Show your child an interesting picture and ask him or her to look at it for a minute. Then turn the picture over and ask your child to list the objects that he or she can remember on a sheet of paper. If you wish, allow your child to look at the picture for another minute to help him or her add more items to the list.

Your child might enjoy reading the following books.

Second-Grade Friends
by Miriam Cohen

Whistle for Willie
by Ezra Jack Keats

The Boxcar Children
by Gertrude Chandler Warner

_____ 's Incentive Chart: Week 5

Name Here

This week, I plan to read _____ minutes each day.

CHART YOUR PROGRESS HERE.

Week 5	Day 1	Day 2	Day 3	Day 4	Day 5
I read for...	minutes	minutes	minutes	minutes	minutes
Put a sticker to show you completed each day's work.					

Congratulations!

Wow! You did a great job this week!

Place sticker here.

Parent or Caregiver's Signature _____

Riddle Fun

Compare *means to look for things that are the same.*
Contrast *means to look for things that are different.*

To solve the riddles in each box, read the clues in the horse.
Then write the letters in the blanks with the matching numbers.

What kind of food does a racehorse like to eat?
___ ___ ___ ___   ___ ___ ___ ___
11   5   10   3   11   9   9   2

1. What letter is in LOG, but not in DOG?
2. What letter is in DIME, but not in TIME?
3. What letter is in BITE, but not in BIKE?
4. What letter is in WEST, but not in REST?
5. What letter is in FAN, but not in FUN?
6. What letter is in BOX, but not in FOX?
7. What letter is in CAR, but not in CAN?
8. What letter is in ME, but not in MY?
9. What letter is in SOCK, but not in SACK?
10. What letter is in SEE, but not in BEE?
11. What letter is in FULL, but not in PULL?

What does a rose sleep in at night?
___ ___ ___ ___ ___ ___   ___ ___ ___
11   1   9   4   8   7   6   8   2

Camp Fiddlestick

 A telling sentence is called a **statement**. *An asking sentence is called a* **question**.
Now ask yourself:

How do sentences begin? How do statements end? How do questions end?

Write three statements and three questions about the picture.

Statements:

1. _____

2. _____

3. _____

Questions:

1. _____

2. _____

3. _____

Sort It Out!

Put each word from the Word Box in the circle where it belongs. We did the first one for you.

Word Box

~~ask~~	funny	short
brother	said	children
pretty	brown	took
purple	say	sister
read	school	while

People, Places, and Things

(nouns)

_____

_____

_____

_____

_____

Action Words

(verbs)

ask

_____

_____

_____

_____

Describing Words

(adjectives)

_____

_____

_____

_____

_____

Snuggle Up With a Book

Day of the Week	Reading Minutes
Sunday	97
Monday	28
Tuesday	73
Wednesday	44
Thursday	51
Friday	45
Saturday	80

Use the chart to answer the questions.

A. What day did Alex read for the longest time?

_____

B. How many minutes did Alex read on Wednesday and Friday? _____ minutes

C. What day did Alex read for the shortest time?

_____

D. How many more minutes did Alex read on Sunday than Tuesday? _____ minutes

E. How many minutes did Alex read on Monday and Thursday? _____ minutes

F. How many more minutes did Alex read on Tuesday than Thursday? _____ minutes

 One hour is 60 minutes. On what days did Alex read longer than one hour?

_____, _____, _____

Scholastic Teaching Resources   Get Ready for 2nd Grade

Number Words

Trace and write.

1 one

2 two

3 three

4 four

5 five

More Number Words

Trace and write.

6 six

7 seven

8 eight

9 nine

10 ten

Scholastic Teaching Resources   Get Ready for 2nd Grade

Money Matters

Alex asked his little brother Billy to trade piggy banks.

Alex's bank has these coins: Billy's has these coins:

Do you think this is a fair trade? _____

Test your answer:

Add up Alex's coins: _____

Add up Billy's coins: _____

Write the totals in this Greater Than/Less Than equation:

_____ > _____

Who has more money? _____

-ill Words

Unscramble each word. Write it on the line.

blil _____

lhil _____

ildrl _____

irlgl _____

lwil _____

liqul _____

lichl _____

lsil _____

Find and circle each word from the Word Bank.

```
t c l h l h f q u i l l s p x f h t h f
c h i l l u y l l b l h i l l t h f h l
c x f h d r i l l t h h f g r i l l s p
s i l l s l p l f c l h h b i l l j k y
t l h f w i l l u c b v b l t h r i l l
u l b l j k y v l c l h l b l m i l l u
```

Word Bank

bill	mill
chill	quill
drill	sill
grill	thrill
hill	will

Write a sentence using one of the –ill family words.

_____

_____

Scholastic Teaching Resources   Get Ready for 2nd Grade

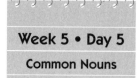

People, Places, and Things

Common nouns name people, places, or things.

Read each sentence. Circle the common nouns.

1. The boy made a boat.

2. The brothers went to the park.

3. A girl was with her grandmother.

4. Two boats crashed in the lake.

5. Friends used a needle and thread
    to fix the sail.

Write the common nouns you circled under the correct heading below.

People	**Places**	**Things**
_____	_____	_____
_____	_____	_____
_____		_____
_____		_____
_____		_____

Story Comprehension

Read the story. Then answer each question.
Fill in the bubble next to the best answer.

> Cats and dogs are good pets. You can find these pets in many homes.
>
> A cat is a good pet. A cat can run and jump. A cat can play with a ball of yarn. A cat can also lick your hand.
>
> A dog is a good pet, too. A dog can chase after a ball. A dog can jump up and catch a stick. A dog can also help keep you safe.

1. What two animals make good pets?
   - O cats
   - O dogs and sharks
   - O dogs and cats

2. What is a good title (name) for this story?
   - O Good Pets
   - O Cats at Home
   - O Pet Food

3. What can both cats and dogs do?
   - O jump up and catch a stick
   - O keep you safe
   - O run and jump

Scholastic Teaching Resources *Get Ready for 2nd Grade*

Helping Your Child Get Ready: Week 6

These are the skills your child will be working on this week.

Math
- graphing
- simple fractions

Reading
- finding the main idea
- reading for details

Writing
- writing to a prompt

Vocabulary
- word categories
- -ink word family

Grammar
- nouns as subjects
- capitalizing proper nouns

Handwriting
- manuscript shapes

Here are some activities you and your child might enjoy.

What's in the Bag? Before putting groceries away, have your child sort the items into categories and explain why he or she decided to group things in a certain way. This activity will help your child understand similarities and differences, as well as exercise descriptive skills.

What's in a Label? Show examples of food labels to your child. Can he or she find a picture and some numbers on the label? Ask: *What do they tell you?*

Two's Company Ask your child to look around and find things that comes in a group, such as twos, fives, or tens.

Shopping List Maker Invite your child to become your official shopping list maker. Dictate to him or her all the items you'll need to purchase on your next grocery store visit. This is a great way to build spelling skills.

Your child might enjoy reading the following books.

Cam Jansen and the Mystery of the Carnival Prize
by David A. Adler

Arthur's New Puppy
by Mark Brown

The Littles
by John Peterson

_____'s Incentive Chart: Week 6

Name Here

This week, I plan to read _____ minutes each day.

CHART YOUR PROGRESS HERE.

Week 6	Day 1	Day 2	Day 3	Day 4	Day 5
I read for...	minutes	minutes	minutes	minutes	minutes
Put a sticker to show you completed each day's work.					

Congratulations!

Wow! You did a great job this week!

#1

Place sticker here.

Parent or Caregiver's Signature _____

Kinds of Groups

Read each sentence. Write the correct word from the box to complete the sentence.

clothing	flower	dessert	tool
number	shape	animal	dish

1. A ⌣ is a kind of _____.

2. A ✿ is a kind of _____.

3. A 🧥 is a kind of _____.

4. A 🧁 is a kind of _____.

5. A 🐔 is a kind of _____.

6. A △ is a kind of _____.

7. A 🔨 is a kind of _____.

8. A **6** is a kind of _____.

 Read the words in the box again. Think of another example for each group.

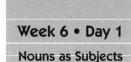
Nouns in Sentences

The **subject** of a sentence is usually a noun.

Choose a word from the tent to use as the subject of each sentence.

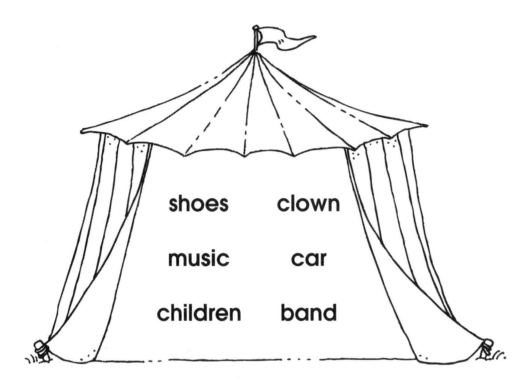

shoes   clown

music   car

children   band

1. The _____ sit on the benches in the tent.

2. A small _____ drives into the ring.

3. This funny _____ jumps out.

4. His big _____ flop.

5. The _____ strikes up a tune.

6. Lively _____ fills the tent.

Write a sentence of your own. Use one of the nouns from the tent as the subject.

_____

_____

Call the Police!

It is good to know that you can call a police officer when you need help. You should not be afraid of the police. Their job is to help people. Police officers help find lost children. They direct traffic when there is a problem on the roads. They arrest criminals so that our towns are safe. When people have been in car accidents, police officers come quickly to help them. During floods, fires, and tornadoes, they take people to safe places. Sometimes they rescue people who are in danger. Police officers have saved many lives. Think of a police officer as your best friend!

What do you think the main idea of this story is? To find out, read the letters that are connected in the puzzle. Write the letters in order beside the matching shapes.

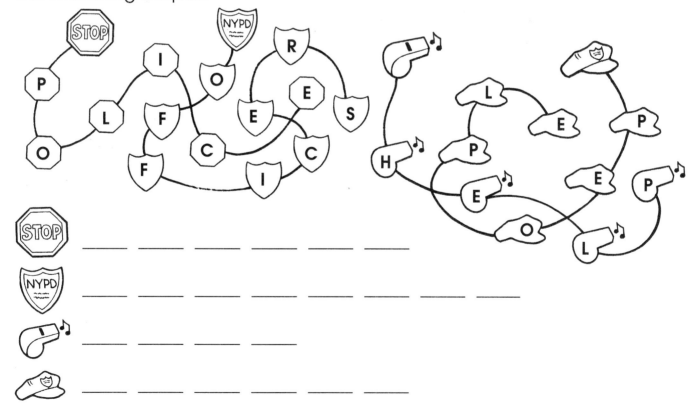

My Favorite Sport

What is your favorite sport? In the box, draw a picture of you playing your favorite sport.

Write three things you know about your favorite sport. Use the words in the word bank if you need help.

1. _____

_____

2. _____

_____

3. _____

_____

Scholastic Teaching Resources   *Get Ready for 2nd Grade*

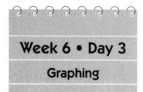

Five Senses

We learn about the world by using our 5 senses. The 5 senses are seeing, hearing, smelling, touching, and tasting.

Look at the pictures on the left side of the graph. Think about which of your senses you use to learn about it. Draw a checkmark in the box to show the senses used. (Hint: You might use more than one.)

	See	Hear	Smell	Touch	Taste
(rooster)					
(sun)					
(drink)					
(flowers)					
(drum)					

Now graph how many senses you used for each object.

5					
4					
3					
2					
1					

(rooster) (sun) (drink) (flowers) (drum)

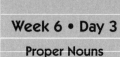
Capitalize Names and Places

Special names of people and places always begin with capital letters. They are called **proper nouns.**

Read the postcard. Find the proper nouns. Write them correctly on the lines below.

Dear sue,

It's very hot here in california. We visited the city of los angeles. Then we swam in the pacific ocean. I miss you.

Love,
tonya

sue wong
11 shore road
austin, texas 78728

1. _____   2. _____

3. _____   4. _____

5. _____   6. _____

7. _____   8. _____

Write a sentence with a proper noun. Underline the capital letter or letters in the proper noun. Then write whether it names a person or a place.

_____

_____

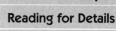
Gorillas

 Details *are parts of a story. Details help you understand what the story is about.*

Gorillas are the largest apes. They live in the rainforests of Africa. Every morning, they wake up and eat a breakfast of leaves, fruit, and bark. During most of the day, the adult gorillas take naps. Meanwhile, young gorillas play. They wrestle and chase each other. They swing on vines. When the adults wake up, everyone eats again. When there is danger, gorillas stand up on their hind legs, scream, and beat their chests. Every night before it gets dark, the gorillas build a new nest to sleep in. They break off leafy branches to make their beds, either on the ground or in the trees. Baby gorillas snuggle up to their mothers to sleep.

Find the answers to the puzzle in the story. Write the answers in the squares with the matching numbers.

Across

1. During the day, adult gorillas _____.

3. Gorillas eat leaves, bark, and _____.

5. The largest apes are _____.

7. In danger, gorillas beat their _____.

8. Young gorillas swing on _____.

Down

2. The continent where gorillas live is _____.

4. When young gorillas play, they _____ and chase each other.

6. Baby gorillas snuggle up to their mothers to _____.

 On another piece of paper, write two things gorillas do that people also do.

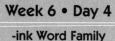
-ink Words

Unscramble each word. Write it on the line.

sikn _____   rnki _____

knwi _____   hkint _____

dknri _____   nstki _____

nlik _____   kinp _____

Find and circle each word from the Word Bank.

s p x f h t h i n k t h f s t i n k y l

r e p i n k s p x f h s i n k t h c h f

t h f w i n k u y v b j k c h b n k i y

d r i n k s p b j k h s h r i n k t h f

u y v b j k b l s l i n k t h f l i n k

k b n k j k t h f r i n k s p x f n k h

Word Bank

drink   sink

link   slink

pink   stink

rink   think

shrink   wink

Write a sentence using one of the –ink family words.

_____

_____

_____

74

Shapes

Trace and write.

oval

heart

circle

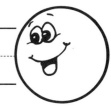

square

triangle

diamond

rectangle

Parts to Color

A fraction has two numbers. The top number will tell you how many parts to color. The bottom number tells you how many parts there are.

Color 1/5 of the circle.   Color 4/5 of the rectangle.

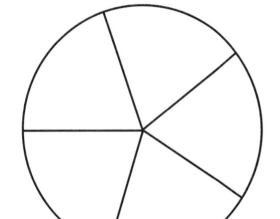   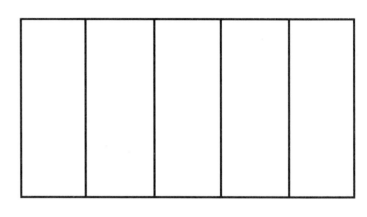

Color 3/5 of the ants.   Color 2/5 of the spiders.

   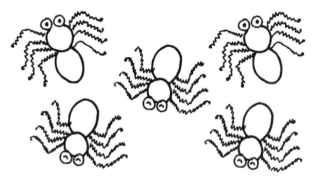

Color 0/5 of the bees.   Color 5/5 of the worms.

   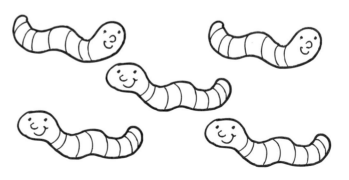

Scholastic Teaching Resources   Get Ready for 2nd Grade

Helping Your Child Get Ready: Week 7

These are the skills your child will be working on this week.

Math
- telling time
- adding 2-digit numbers without regrouping

Reading
- real or fantasy
- sequencing

Writing
- writing to a prompt

Vocabulary
- long vowels
- -ock word family

Grammar
- plural nouns

Handwriting
- manuscript days of the week

Here are some activities you and your child might enjoy.

Who Is It? Play a guessing game. Give your child clues about someone your family knows. Can he or she guess this person's identity? Trade places. Play again.

What's My Sign? When you go places with your child, ask him or her to look around and record as many signs and symbols as possible and then share the list. Discuss why some road signs do not have words and others do. Encourage your child to make up his or her own "road signs" to post around your home.

Two-Minute Lists Give your child two minutes to list as many plural words as he or she can think of that end with the letter *s*.

Summer Games Plan a mini "Summer Olympics" with your family. Play classic picnic games such as a water-balloon toss or a three-legged race, or make up fun games of your own. Take turns trying them!

Your child might enjoy reading the following books.

Cloudy With a Chance of Meatballs
by Judi Barrett

Horrible Harry in Room 2B
by Suzy Kline

Cookie's Week
by Cindy Ward

_____'s Incentive Chart: Week 7
Name Here

This week, I plan to read _____ minutes each day.

CHART YOUR PROGRESS HERE.

Week 7	Day 1	Day 2	Day 3	Day 4	Day 5
I read for...	minutes	minutes	minutes	minutes	minutes
Put a sticker to show you completed each day's work.					

 # Congratulations!

Wow! You did a great job this week!

Place sticker here.

Parent or Caregiver's Signature _____

Days of the Week

Trace and write.

Sunday

Monday

Tuesday

Wednesday

Thursday

Friday

Saturday

Picture Maze

Can you get to the end of this maze?
Say the picture names. Listen for the sound of long *a*.
Color the picture if the name has the long-*a* sound.

Start

fence	bicycle	leaf	tube	hose	pipe
cane	coat	snail	safe	plane	lion
tic-tac-toe	rake	tray	pie	glue	cake
bride	bone	kite	3	10	hay
jeep	cats	weather vane	nail	sheep	diving
dime	goat	chain	vase	flute	pail

Finish

Scholastic Teaching Resources   *Get Ready for 2nd Grade*

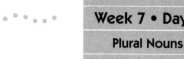
More Than One

Many nouns, or naming words, add **-s** to show more than one.

Read the sets of sentences. Draw a line under the sentence that has a naming word that names more than one.

1. Jan has her mittens.

   Jan has her mitten.

2. She will run up a hill.

   She will run up hills.

3. Jan runs with her dogs.

   Jan runs with her dog.

4. The dogs can jump.

   The dog can jump.

Look at each picture. Read each word. Write the plural naming word that matches the picture.

5.  _____

   cat _____

6.  _____

   sock _____

Fun at the Farm

 Story events that can really happen are **real**. *Story events that are make-believe are* **fantasy**.

Read each sentence below. If it could be real, color the picture. If it is make-believe, put an X on the picture.

 Dairy cows give milk.

 The farmer planted pizza and hamburgers.

 The pig said, "Let's go to the dance tonight!"

 The mouse ate the dinner table.

 The hay was stacked in the barn.

 The newborn calf walked with wobbly legs.

 The green tractor ran out of gas.

 Two crickets sang "Mary Had a Little Lamb."

 The goat and the sheep got married by the big tree.

 Rain made the roads muddy.

 Four little ducks swam in the pond.

 The farmer's family ate a pie.

 On another sheet of paper, write one make-believe sentence about the farmer's house and one real sentence about it.

More Than One

A **plural** noun names more than one person, place, or thing.
To make most nouns plural, add an **-s**.

Study the picture. Read the words. Write the plural of the word if there is more than one in the picture.

One	More Than One	One	More Than One
1. girl	_____	7. ball	_____
2. boy	_____	8. hoop	_____
3. doll	_____	9. man	_____
4. lion	_____	10. cap	_____
5. poster	_____	11. shirt	_____
6. balloon	_____	12. hand	_____

Write a sentence using one of the plural nouns.

_____

_____

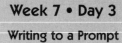

All About Ice Cream

 Draw the tallest ice cream cone you can in the box.

Write three things you know about ice cream. Use the words in the word bank if you need help.

1.

   _____

2.

   _____

3.

   _____

```
···· WORD BANK ········

   cold        tasty

   flavors     cone

   colors      chocolate

   melts       vanilla

   sweet       yummy
```

If you could invent an ice cream flavor, what would it be?

_____

_____

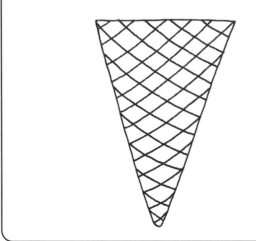

Scholastic Teaching Resources   *Get Ready for 2nd Grade*

Counting on Good Manners

Add. Then use the code to write a letter in each oval to find the "good manner" words.

11 + 10	62 + 31	44 + 34	41 + 5	13 + 31	35 + 43

◯ ◯ ◯ ◯ ◯ ◯

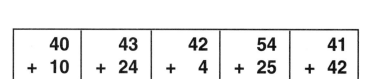

May I have some candy, please?

40 + 10	43 + 24	42 + 4	54 + 25	41 + 42

◯ ◯ ◯ ◯ ◯

57 + 2	22 + 3	34 + 32

◯ ◯ ◯

54 + 5	21 + 4	41 + 25	21 + 11	26 + 52

◯ ◯ ◯ ' ◯ ◯

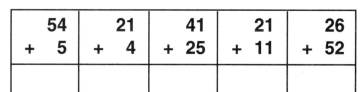

Thank you!

50 + 30	70 + 8	50 + 43	11 + 7	15 + 10	31 + 4	17 + 61

◯ ◯ ◯ ◯ ◯ ◯ ◯

Code

18 C	21 P	25 O	32 R	35 M	44 S	46 A	50 T
59 Y	66 U	67 H	78 E	79 N	80 W	83 K	93 L

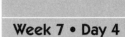

-ock Words

Unscramble each word. Write it on the line.

crko _____   kfcol _____

skoc _____   okknc _____

cosmk _____   cclok _____

olkc _____   dkoc _____

Find and circle each word from the Word Bank.

```
s p b j k x f h r o c k u c h y u v b l
l o c k u y c k v c k b l f l o c k i y
t h c k b j k h f k n o c k t h c k i f
f r o c k s p x b j k f h s o c k t h f
c l o c k t c h h c k f d o c k x f c k
t b j k h f c r o c k s p h s m o c k k
```

Word Bank

clock	knock
crock	lock
dock	rock
flock	smock
frock	sock

Write a sentence using one of the –ock family words.

_____

_____

A Pencil Sandwich?

How does the lead get inside a wooden pencil? Pencils are made out of strips of wood cut from cedar trees. Then grooves are cut in the strips. Graphite is laid into the grooves. (We call it lead, but it is really graphite.) Then another strip of wood is glued on top of the first one, making a pencil sandwich! The wood is rounded in rows on the top strip of wood and the bottom strip. Then the pencils are cut apart and painted. An eraser is added on the end and held in place by a metal ring. When you buy a pencil, you sharpen it, and then you are ready to write.

Look at the pictures. Number them in the order that they happen in the story.

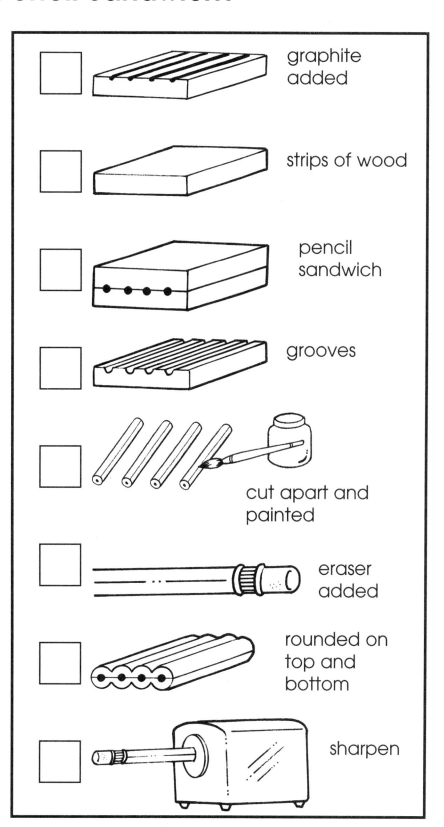

graphite added

strips of wood

pencil sandwich

grooves

cut apart and painted

eraser added

rounded on top and bottom

sharpen

Clock Work

Draw the hands on the clock so it shows 4:00.

Draw the hands on the clock so it shows 4:30.

What do you do at 4:00 in the afternoon? Write about it on the lines below.

_____

_____

Draw the hands on the clock so it shows 6:00.

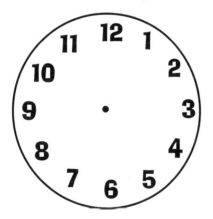

Draw the hands on the clock so it shows 6:30.

What do you do at 6:00 in the evening? Write about it on the lines below.

_____

_____

Scholastic Teaching Resources   Get Ready for 2nd Grade

Helping Your Child Get Ready: Week 8

These are the skills your child will be working on this week.

Math
- subtracting 2-digit numbers without regrouping
- regrouping review: ones and tens

Reading
- classifying
- making predictions

Vocabulary
- long and short vowels
- -ump word family

Grammar
- verbs

Handwriting
- manuscript months of the year

Here are some activities you and your child might enjoy.

Less Is More Provide your child with a reclosable bag containing 25 pennies, 5 nickels, and 1 quarter. Encourage him or her to count the pennies by arranging them into groups of 5. Explain that a quarter is worth 25 cents and 5 nickels also equals 25 cents. Ask questions such as *How many pennies are in a nickel? Which is worth more: 75 pennies or 4 quarters?*

Simon Says This favorite game can be used to practice a specific skill or concept such as prepositions. For example, say *Simon says, "Put your hands* behind *your back,"* or *Simon says, "Walk* across *the room,"* or *Put your palm* under *your chin.* Remind your child to follow instructions only when "Simon Says."

Sidewalk Chalkboard Your child may find practicing spelling words or handwriting more like play when using colorful sidewalk chalk outdoors. Challenge your child to write words as big as possible, then as small as possible.

Surprise Story Cut out ten pictures from a magazine. Put them in a bag. Invite your child to take them out one at a time to tell a story.

Your child might enjoy reading the following books.

The Art Lesson
by Tomie dePaola

A House Is a House for Me
by Mary Ann Hoberman

If You Give a Pig a Pancake
by Laura Numeroff

_____ **'s Incentive Chart: Week 8**
Name Here

This week, I plan to read_____ minutes each day.

CHART YOUR PROGRESS HERE.

Week 8	Day 1	Day 2	Day 3	Day 4	Day 5
I read for...	minutes	minutes	minutes	minutes	minutes
Put a sticker to show you completed each day's work.					

Congratulations!

Wow! You did a great job this week!

Place sticker here.

Parent or Caregiver's Signature _____

Color the Bowtie

Do the subtraction problems in the picture below.
Then use the Color Key to tell you what color to
make each answer.

Color Key

14 = red   47 = yellow

26 = purple   63 = green

33 = blue

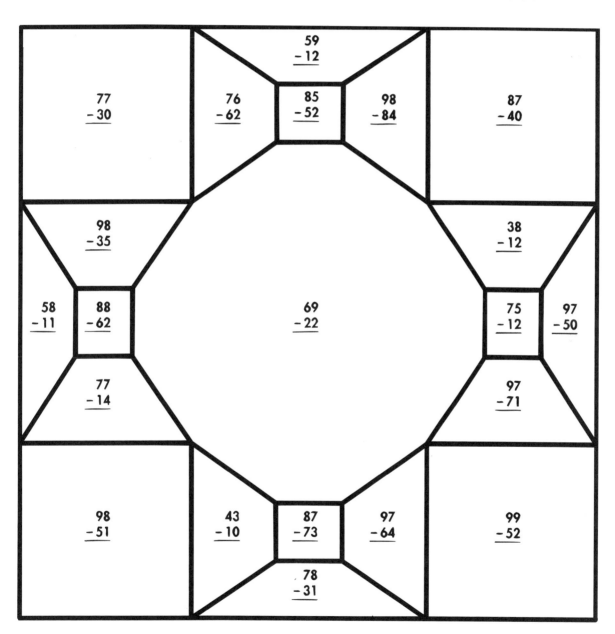

On another sheet of paper, draw a picture of four of your friends or
family members. Give each one a bowtie!

What's Missing?

Something is missing from each picture. Read the clues and look at the pictures carefully to find out what it is. Say the name of each missing item and add it to the picture.

1.
Clue: long *i*
You fly it.

2.
Clue: short *i*
You play on it.

3.
Clue: long *a*
You put flowers in it.

4.
Clue: short *a*
You hit a ball with it.

5.
Clue: long *e*
You need two.

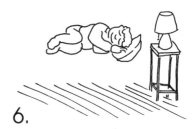

6.
Clue: short *e*
You sleep on it.

7.
Clue: long *o*
You drive on it.

8.
Clue: short *o*
You wear it on your foot.

9.
Clue: short *u*
You drink from it.

Scholastic Teaching Resources   Get Ready for 2nd Grade

Months

Trace and write.

January

February

March

April

May

June

Months

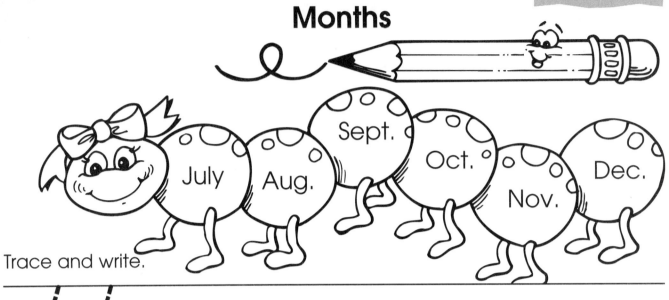

Trace and write.

July

August

September

October

November

December

Scholastic Teaching Resources   *Get Ready for 2nd Grade*

Summer Vacation

Grouping like things together helps you see how parts of a story are connected and makes the story easier to understand.

Last summer, Dad, Mom, Tim, and Tara went to the beach in Florida. They swam, fished, built sandcastles, and went sailing. Mom brought a picnic lunch. She spread a blanket on the sand and set out ham sandwiches, potato chips, apples, and cookies. She brought lemonade in the cooler. Later, Tim and Tara walked along the beach and saw a crab walking sideways. A stray dog was barking at it. A starfish had washed up on the beach, too. Tim threw bread crumbs up in the air to feed a flock of seagulls. Then the family went back to the hotel, and Tim and Tara played video games until bedtime.

Use the story to find the answers. Fill in the blanks.

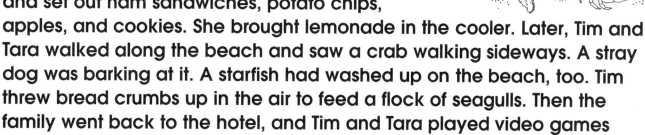

People Who Went to the Beach

Picnic Items

Living Things They Saw on the Beach

What They Did

A Great Catch

Circle each group of 10. Write the number of tens and ones on the chart.
Then write the number on the baseball glove.

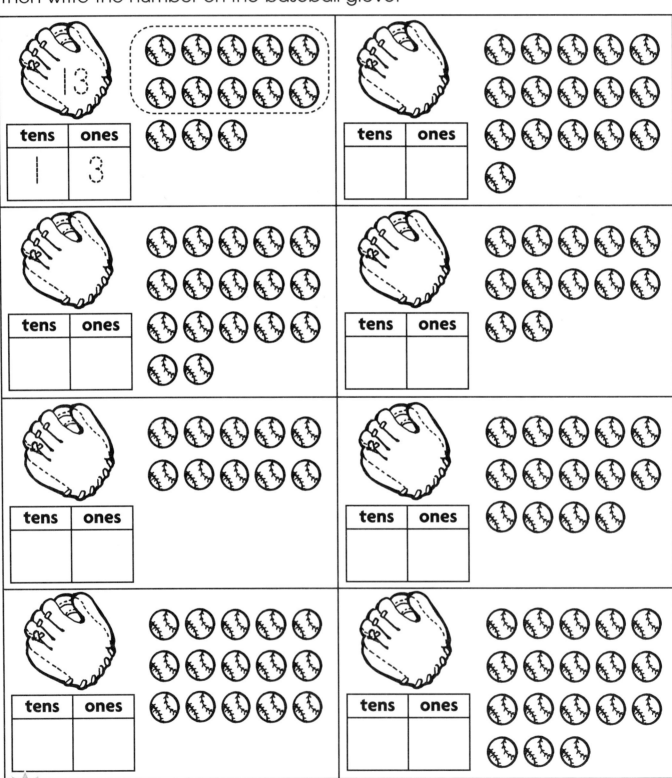

Scholastic Teaching Resources   Get Ready for 2nd Grade

Will He Be All Right?

➡️ *Use story details to guess what will happen next.*

Father Eagle said to his young son, "Today is a very special day. You will fly for the first time." Baby Eagle was afraid. He said, "But Father, I don't know how. What should I do?" His father laid a strong wing on his little shoulder and said, "You will know." They stood at the edge of a very high cliff. Far below were huge rocks and a canyon. "Ride the wind, my son!" said Father Eagle, and he gently pushed his son off the cliff. Baby Eagle yelled, "Help! Help!" and wildly flapped his wings. All of a sudden something wonderful happened!

1. What do you think happened next? Color the rock that tells the most likely answer.

2. Why did you choose that answer? Find the sentence in the story that gives you a hint that the story has a happy ending. Write it here.

_____

_____

Unscramble the words and write the answer: **ODPRU**   **AARDFI**

3. How do you think Baby Eagle felt at first when he was pushed off the cliff? _____

4. How do you think Father Eagle felt at the end of the story? _____

Action at Practice

A **verb** is an action word. It tells what someone or something is doing.

Read each sentence. Write the action verb in the telling part of the sentence.

1. Ronald runs to the field. _____

2. Michael wears a batting helmet. _____

3. He smacks the ball hard. _____

4. Ronald holds the wrong end
   of the bat. _____

5. He misses the ball. _____

6. Ronald waits in left field. _____

7. He writes G for great. _____

8. Ronald's father helps him. _____

Write a sentence about the picture.
Use an action verb and circle it.

_____

_____

_____

Scholastic Teaching Resources   *Get Ready for 2nd Grade*

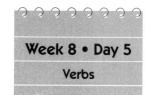

Action at the Game

A **verb** is an action word. It tells what someone or something is doing.

Draw a line to match each sentence with an action verb. Then write the action verbs on the lines to finish the sentences.

1. Moms and dads _____ the game.   throws

2. The pitcher _____ the ball.   opens

3. Ronald _____ his eyes.   watch

4. The team _____ for Ronald.   cheers

5. Ronald _____ the ball past the pitcher.   runs

6. He _____ to first base.   hits

7 Someone _____, "Go, Ronald, go!"   eat

8. The kids _____ ice cream after the game.   yells

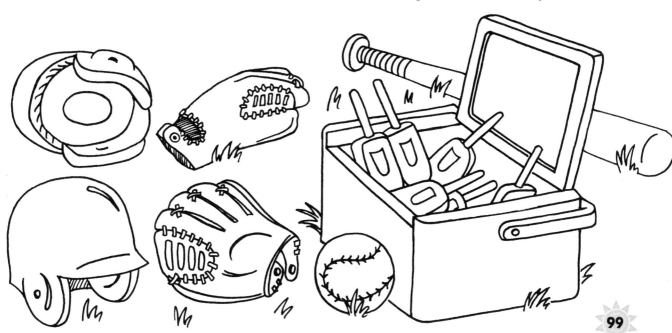

Scholastic Teaching Resources   Get Ready for 2nd Grade

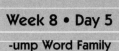
-ump Words

Unscramble each word. Write it on the line.

mpbu _____   mphu _____

rupmg _____   ppum _____

pjum _____   muppl _____

umpst _____   mpdu _____

Find and circle each word from the Word Bank.

u y c h v b l s t u m p s p x p l u m p

f h u m p u c h y v f h b l j u m p p m

o p g m h b u m p m p c h g r u m p s t

j s d b n h k m p p u m p s p m p x f h

d u m p t h c h f c l u m p w s p x f h

t c m p e r c a b t h j k h h f l u m p

Word Bank

bump	jump
clump	lump
dump	plump
grump	pump
hump	stump

Write a sentence using one of the –ump family words.

_____

_____

_____

Scholastic Teaching Resources   Get Ready for 2nd Grade

Helping Your Child Get Ready: Week 9

These are the skills your child will be working on this week.

Math
- adding or subtracting with regrouping

Reading
- developing vocabulary using context clues
- identifying cause and effect

Writing
- descriptive words
- writing to a prompt

Vocabulary
- consonant blends
- -unk word family

Grammar
- past-tense verbs

Here are some activities you and your child might enjoy.

Give Me a Foot! Cut two pieces of yarn or string to 12 inches long. Give the yarn to your child and ask him or her to find something shorter than 12 inches and one thing longer than 12 inches. Can your child find something that is exactly 12 inches? Challenge your child to find something that is 24 inches!

Summer Fun Ask your child to list things he or she loves about summer and then write them on paper, one word on each line. Your child has made a list poem! Encourage your child to give it a title and read it aloud to the family.

ABC Order Read a list of 5–7 words to your child, such as the days of the week or the ingredients to a tasty sandwich. Then have him or her put the words in alphabetical order.

Listen and Draw Describe an object, animal, or person to your child and ask him or her to draw it. How close does the drawing come to looking like the real thing? Then, ask him or her to describe something for you to draw.

Your child might enjoy reading the following books.

Click, Clack, Moo Cows That Type
by Betsy Lewis

The Day Jimmy's Boa Ate the Wash
by Trisha Hakes Noble

The True Story of the Three Little Pigs
by Jon Scieszka

_____'s Incentive Chart: Week 9
Name Here

This week, I plan to read _____ minutes each day.

CHART YOUR PROGRESS HERE.

Week 9	Day 1	Day 2	Day 3	Day 4	Day 5
I read for...	minutes	minutes	minutes	minutes	minutes
Put a sticker to show you completed each day's work.					

Congratulations!
Wow! You did a great job this week!

#1

Place sticker here.

Parent or Caregiver's Signature _____

Don't Forget Your Keys

Add. Then follow the clue to find the right key. Write the sum in the key hole.

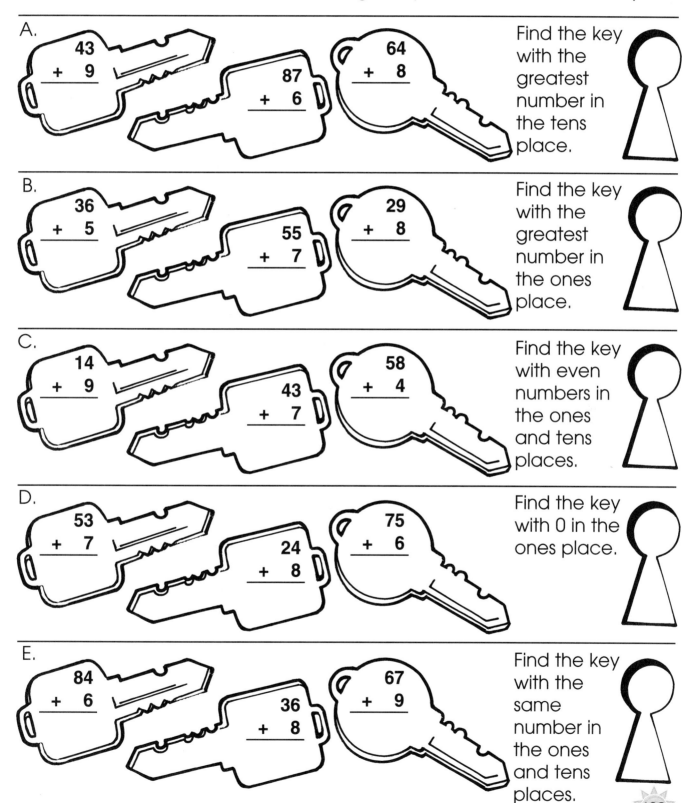

A.
$$43 + 9$$
$$87 + 6$$
$$64 + 8$$

Find the key with the greatest number in the tens place.

B.
$$36 + 5$$
$$55 + 7$$
$$29 + 8$$

Find the key with the greatest number in the ones place.

C.
$$14 + 9$$
$$43 + 7$$
$$58 + 4$$

Find the key with even numbers in the ones and tens places.

D.
$$53 + 7$$
$$24 + 8$$
$$75 + 6$$

Find the key with 0 in the ones place.

E.
$$84 + 6$$
$$36 + 8$$
$$67 + 9$$

Find the key with the same number in the ones and tens places.

What Happened?

Some verbs add **-ed** to tell about actions that happened in the past. Find the past-tense verb in each sentence. Write it on the line.

1. Last spring, Daisy planted a garden. _____

2. Floyd watered the garden. _____

3. Together they weeded their garden. _____

4. One day they discovered a big carrot. _____

Read each sentence. If the sentence has a past-tense verb, write it on the line. If the sentence does not have a past-tense verb, leave the line blank.

5. They like to eat carrots. _____

6. They pulled on the carrot. _____

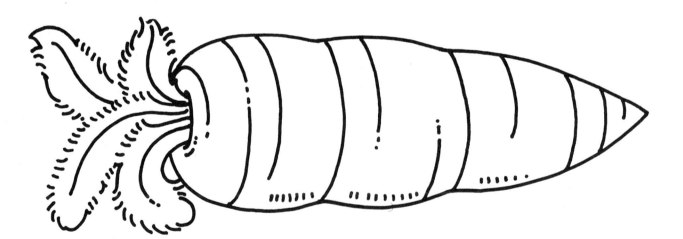

Scholastic Teaching Resources   *Get Ready for 2nd Grade*

What Else Happened?

Some verbs add **-ed** to tell about actions that happened in the past.

Read the first sentence in each pair. Change the underlined verb to tell about the past.

1. Today my dogs <u>push</u> open the back door.

    Yesterday my dogs _____ open the back door.

2. Today they <u>splash</u> in the rain puddles.

    Last night they _____ in the rain puddles.

3. Now they <u>roll</u> in the mud.

    Last week they _____ in the mud.

4. Today I <u>follow</u> my dogs' footprints.

    Last Sunday I _____ my dogs' footprints.

5. Now I <u>wash</u> my dogs from head to toe.

    Earlier I _____ my dogs from head to toe.

Write a sentence using one of the verbs you wrote.

_____

_____

Blends Game

Say the words.

Listen for the beginning sounds.

Use the Beginning Sounds Color Code to make a picture.

Beginning Sounds Color Code

bl = blue	cl = red	fl = yellow	gl = green	pl = brown	sl = purple

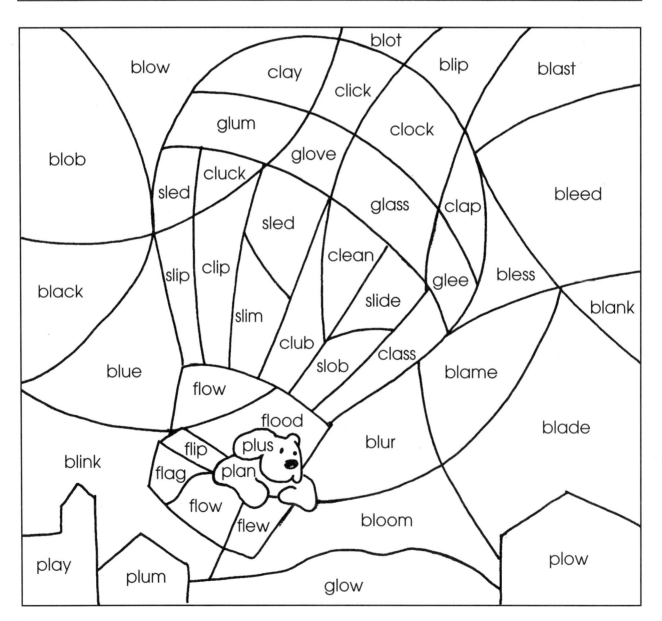

Scholastic Teaching Resources   *Get Ready for 2nd Grade*

Busy as a Bee

Bees are hardworking insects. They live together in a nest called a <u>hive</u>. There is one <u>queen bee</u> in each hive. She is the largest bee. There are hundreds of <u>worker bees</u>. The worker bees fly from flower to flower gathering a sweet liquid called <u>nectar</u>. They make honey from the nectar and store it in little rooms in the hive. Each little room is a <u>cell</u>. Many cells in a row make a <u>honeycomb</u>. When a bear or a person tries to steal the honey, the bees swarm, flying around in large groups. Each bee has a <u>stinger</u> to protect it from its enemies. A person who is a <u>beekeeper</u> makes wooden hives for bees, then sells the honey when the bees finish making it.

Look at the picture below. Use each underlined word in the story to label the pictures.

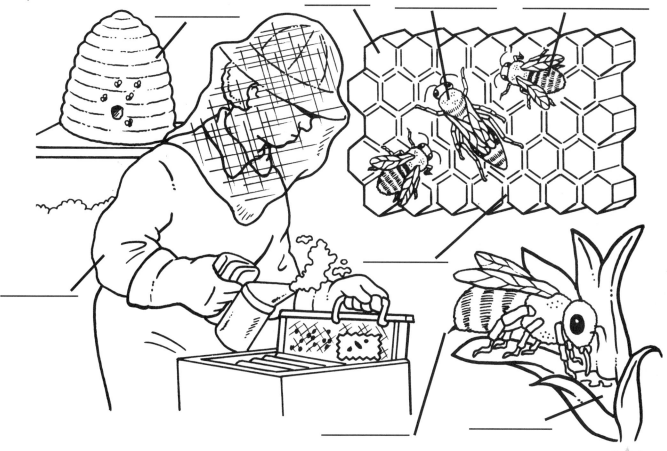

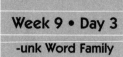
-unk Words

Unscramble each word. Write it on the line.

ntrku _____   nkbu _____

uhcnk _____   knsrhu _____

knksu _____   uskn _____

khun _____   nskut _____

Find and circle each word from the Word Bank.

m n s k u n k s p x h h u n k s p x f h

h k v b l t r u n k k m n u y i c n b h

k n k m s u n k s p x f h b u n k k m n

u y c h b l s t u n k s p k x f h n j k

k j u n k t h f d u n k k m p x n k m n

m n c h u n k u y c h l c h s h r u n k

Word Bank

bunk	shrunk
chunk	skunk
dunk	stunk
hunk	sunk
junk	trunk

Write a sentence using one of the –unk family words.

_____

_____

_____

Digging Up Bones

Help Daisy find a delicious bone! Subtract.
Circle the answer that goes with each bone.

> is greater than and < is less than

A.
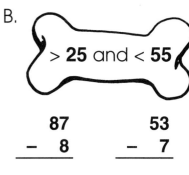

> **40** and < **70**

56	94
− 8	− 5

B.

> **25** and < **55**

87	53
− 8	− 7

C.

> **37** and < **82**

45	81
− 9	− 5

D.

> **74** and < **96**

83	68
− 6	− 9

E.

> **18** and < **49**

57	23
− 9	− 9

F.
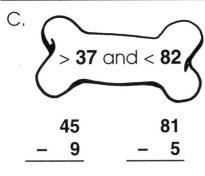

> **63** and < **87**

70	75
− 9	− 7

G.

> **16** and < **56**

23	47
− 9	− 8

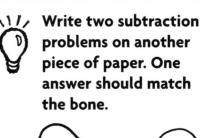

Write two subtraction problems on another piece of paper. One answer should match the bone.

> **48** and < **87**

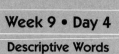
Country Roads

A good sentence uses describing words to help the reader "paint a picture" in his or her mind.

Add a describing word from the list to finish each sentence.

1. The _____ chicken laid

   _____ eggs in her nest.

2. The _____ barn

   keeps the _____

   animals warm at night.

3. _____ carrots grow in

   the _____ garden.

4. Two _____ pigs sleep in

   the _____ pen.

5. The _____ cows drink

   from the _____ pond.

6. A _____ scarecrow

   frightens the _____ birds.

wooden

sunny

lazy

black

three

orange

thirsty

cold

shallow

muddy

funny

fat

On another piece of paper, write three sentences describing your favorite place to visit.

Scholastic Teaching Resources   *Get Ready for 2nd Grade*

An American Volcano

Mount Saint Helens is an active volcano in the state of Washington. In 1980, this volcano erupted, spewing hot lava into the air. Explosions caused a huge cloud of dust. This gray dust filled the air and settled on houses and cars many miles away. The thick dust made it hard for people and animals to breathe. The explosions flattened trees on the side of the mountain. The hot rocks caused forest fires. The snow that was on the mountain melted quickly, causing floods and mud slides. Mount Saint Helens still erupts from time to time but not as badly as it did in 1980.

Read each phrase below. Write the number of each phrase in the explosion of the volcano that correctly completes the sentence.

1. Mount Saint Helens erupted,

2. The thick ash made it hard

3. The explosions

4. The hot rocks caused

5. Melting snow caused

6. Because Mount Saint Helens is an active volcano,

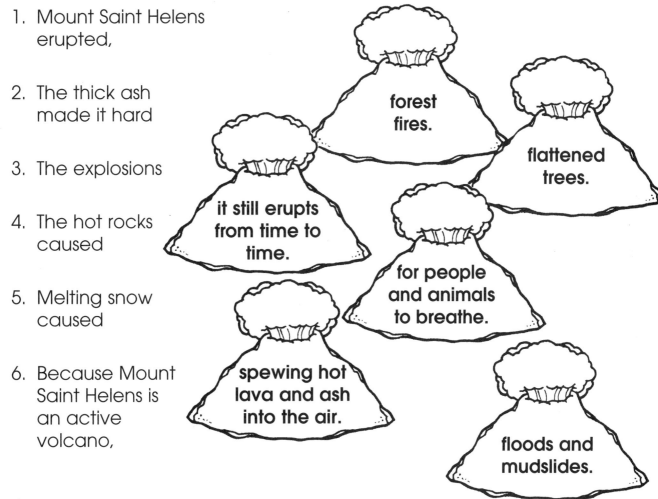

forest fires.

flattened trees.

it still erupts from time to time.

for people and animals to breathe.

spewing hot lava and ash into the air.

floods and mudslides.

Write a story that begins this way:
We were camping in the mountains, when all of a sudden a volcano erupted!

Scholastic Teaching Resources   *Get Ready for 2nd Grade*

Letter to a Friend

Imagine that you are going to write a letter to a friend. Think of questions to ask in the letter. Then, think of something you would like to tell your friend. In the box, draw a picture to show what you wrote about.

Date _____

Dear _____,

How _____?

What _____?

I hope that _____.

Something interesting that happened to me was

_____

_____.

Your friend,

_____

Scholastic Teaching Resources   *Get Ready for 2nd Grade*

Helping Your Child Get Ready: Week 10

These are the skills your child will be working on this week.

Math
- adding with regrouping
- multiplication fact families
- fractions

Reading
- analyzing characters
- comprehension

Writing
- writing to a prompt

Vocabulary
- sight words

Grammar
- identifying nouns
- using nouns and verbs

Handwriting
- manuscript planets

Here are some activities you and your child might enjoy.

Time for Review With your child, find out the time for sunrise and sunset, and determine the current time of day. Ask questions such as *What time will it be in one hour? What time was it one hour ago? What time will it be in 15 minutes? How many hours are there between sunrise and sunset? How many hours are there between sunset and sunrise?*

Imagine That! Invite your child to close his or her eyes. Then ask: *What sounds do you hear?* See if your child can name ten.

Mum's the Word This is a fun dinnertime family game. Agree on a small word that is used frequently in conversation, such as *the* or *and*. This word becomes "mum." No one can say it! Anyone who does, drops out. The last person left is the winner.

Comic Mix-Up Build up your child's sequencing skills. Cut a comic strip into sections. Ask your child to put the strip in the correct order and to explain his or her thinking.

Your child might enjoy reading the following books.

Madeline
by Ludwig Bemelmans

I Spy Treasure Hunt
by Jean Marzollo

How I Spent My Summer Vacation
by Mark Teague

_____'s Incentive Chart: Week 10

Name Here

This week, I plan to read _____ minutes each day.

CHART YOUR PROGRESS HERE.

Week 10	Day 1	Day 2	Day 3	Day 4	Day 5
I read for...	minutes	minutes	minutes	minutes	minutes
Put a sticker to show you completed each day's work.					

Congratulations!

Wow! You did a great job this week!

#1

Place sticker here.

Parent or Caregiver's Signature _____

A Noun Puzzle

A **noun** is a word that names a person, place, or thing.

Can you find the hidden picture?

Use the color code to color the spaces that have nouns.

Color Code

Nouns that name things = orange

Nouns that name places = green

Nouns that name people or animals = blue

Other words = light blue

Write a sentence using one of the nouns you found.

_____

_____

Whales

Read the story. Then answer each question.
Fill in the bubble next to the best answer.

A whale is a very big animal. Whales live in the sea. Some whales swim with each other. They travel in large groups, called pods. They swim around, looking for food.

Whales feed on sea life. Some whales eat plants. Other whales have teeth and can eat seals and small fish.

Whales must stay wet all the time. However, they also must come to the top of the sea to breathe. When a whale leaps out of the water to catch a breath of air, it is an amazing sight.

1. What are pods?
   O whale food
   O groups of whales
   O sea animals

2. What is
   a good title
   (name) for this story?
   O The Sea
   O Fish
   O Whales

3. What must all whales do?
   O eat seals and fish
   O spend time on land
   O stay wet

4. Why do whales sometimes jump out of the water?
   O to warm up
   O to get air
   O to catch fish

Scholastic Teaching Resources   *Get Ready for 2nd Grade*

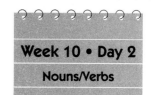

Verb or Noun?

The meaning of a word often depends on how the word is used. Some words can be used as both verbs and nouns.

Add the word at the left to each sentence pair. Write verb or noun on the line next to each sentence to show how you used the word.

peel   1. The _____ is the cover of an orange.   _____

2. The students _____ their oranges.   _____

ride   3. Jan's _____ on the camel was bumpy. _____

4. People _____ on camels in the desert.   _____

color   5. The twins _____ their pictures.   _____

6. That _____ fades in the sun.   _____

smell   7. The men _____ smoke.   _____

8. The _____ of flowers fills the air.   _____

lock   9. The _____ on the box is old.   _____

10. The Turners _____ their door at night.   _____

Write sentences using each of the following words as a verb and a noun: call, ring, turn.

Rocket Riddle

What did the rocket say when it left the party?

What To Do

To find the answer to the riddle, solve the multiplication problems. Then match each product with a letter in the Key below. Write the correct letters on the blanks below.

1. **5 x 1** = _____
2. **8 x 1** = _____
3. **11 x 1** = _____
4. **26 x 1** = _____
5. **3 x 2** = _____

6. **5 x 2** = _____
7. **6 x 2** = _____
8. **8 x 2** = _____
9. **9 x 2** = _____
10. **12 x 2** = _____

Key

10 .... F	27 .... U	20 .... W
13 C	8 .... E	7 .... D
11 .... O	6 .... K	12 .... T
16 .... E	9 .... B	26 .... O
5 .... A	24 .... F	18 .... T

Riddle Answer:

"TIM __ __ __ __ __ __ __ __ __ __."
      8   7 3   9 1 5 2   4 6 10

Scholastic Teaching Resources   Get Ready for 2nd Grade

My Favorite Dentist

A **character** *is a person or animal in a story. To understand a character better, you should pay attention to the details a story often gives about the character.*

Some kids are scared to go to the dentist, but not me. I have a funny dentist. His name is Dr. Smileyface. I don't think that's his real name, but that's what he tells all the kids who come to see him. He has a cool waiting room. It has video games and a big toy box. Dr. Smileyface always wears funny hats. Sometimes he has his face painted. He asks funny questions like "Are you married yet?" and "Do you eat flowers to make your breath smell so sweet?" That makes me laugh. One time, he told me this joke, "What has lots of teeth but never goes to the dentist? A comb!" When I laughed, he pulled my tooth. It didn't hurt at all! He also teaches me how to take care of my teeth because he says he doesn't want me to get a cavity the size of the Grand Canyon. Before I go home, he always gives me a surprise. Last time I went, he gave me a rubber spider to scare my mom with!

Color the pictures that could be Dr. Smileyface. Put an X on the pictures that could not be him.

Draw a line from the toothbrush to the tooth that makes the sentence true.

6. Dr. Smileyface makes

7. The child who wrote this story

8. Dr. Smileyface teaches kids

9. Dr. Smileyface sends kids home

how to take care of their teeth.

his patients laugh.

with a surprise.

is not afraid to go to the dentist.

Sort It Out!

Write each word from the Word Box under the question it can help answer. We did the first one for you.

Word Box

after	~~sister~~	now	there
children	before	school	us
here	men	soon	

Where?
(place words)

_____

_____

_____

Who?
(people words)

sister

_____

_____

_____

When?
(time words)

_____

_____

_____

Scholastic Teaching Resources   *Get Ready for 2nd Grade*

Fractions

A fraction has two numbers. The top number will tell you how many parts to color. The bottom number tells you how many total parts there are.

Color 1/7 of the candy.

Color 4/7 of the candy.

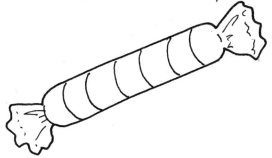

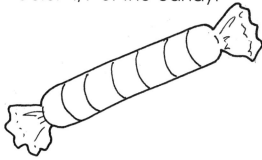

This loaf of bread is cut into 7 slices.

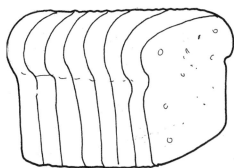

Could you color 8/7 of the bread? _____

Explain your answer. _____

Color 7/7 of the bananas.

Color 3/7 of the peanut butter jars.

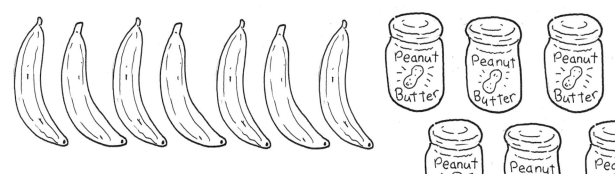

The Planets

Write the names of the planets.

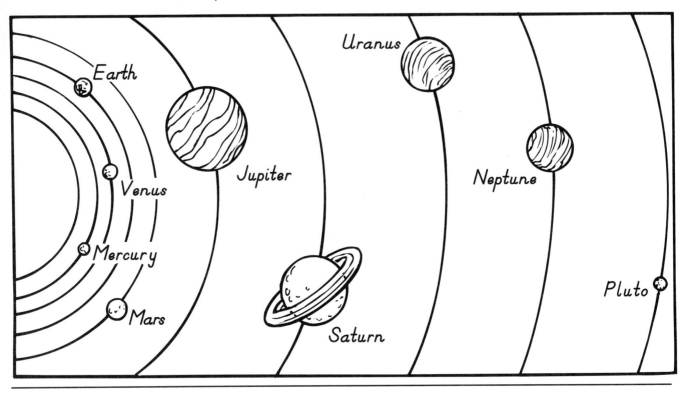

Carnival Fun

Do the problems below. Then find your answers hidden in the carnival scene and circle them. Can you find all twelve answers?

15	27	34	15	16	12
33	23	23	25	14	31
+ 27	+ 12	+ 24	+ 10	+ 14	+ 17

28	43	10	29	37	51
22	27	17	13	31	23
+ 45	+ 27	+ 18	+ 16	+ 17	+ 17

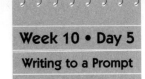

A Summer Memory

 A memory is something you remember. Think of something special that you did over the summer. In the box, draw a picture of your memory.

Word Bank

swimming

riding

playing

bicycle

camp

family

vacation

beach

mountains

visit

fun

happy

proud

excited

In this picture, I am _____

_____

This was special because _____

_____

When I was doing this, I felt _____

Scholastic Teaching Resources   *Get Ready for 2nd Grade*

Page 8
1. Raul
2. Mrs. Chin
3. Sue
4. Lee Park

Page 10
Food: apple, bread, pasta
Toys: doll, ball, game
Colors: yellow, green, red

Page 11
A. 6 + 4 = 10; B. 10 – 5 = 5; C. 9 – 2 = 7;
D. 4 + 6 = 10; E. 7 + 2 = 9; F. 2 + 3 = 5;
G. 5 + 3 = 8; H. 6 + 4 = 10; I. 8 – 7 = 1;
J. 10 – 3 = 7

Page 12
1. This bear likes snow.
2. The water is cold.
3. The bear runs fast.
4. Two bears play.

Page 13
Main idea: Trucks do important work.

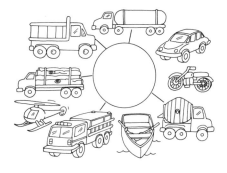

Page 14
Top side of the street: 50, 52, 54, 56
Bottom side of the street: 51, 53, 55
Extra: The even numbers are on one side
of the street. The odd numbers are on
the other side of the street.

Page 15
Kelly packed pajamas, shirt, shorts,
toothbrush, toothpaste, hairbrush,
swimsuit, pillow, storybooks, sunglasses.
Compound words: grandmother,
suitcase, toothbrush, toothpaste,
hairbrush, swimsuit, storybooks, sunglasses

Page 16
plank, bank, tank, crank, drank, stank,
blank, yank

```
p r m b i n a t a n k i o h r s t a n k
c k l b n k d r a n k r n a r t y j h j
i l r b l a n k r i o n a c r a n k e w
k a y a n k i b k r c a r n k y u r k n
n k r n a f l a n k i c y x r p l a n k
u r k n a k b a n k r n i s a n k v a k
```

Page 19
1. ten; 2. net; 3. tub; 4. bus; 5. sun;
6. nut; 7. top; 8. pan

Page 20
sweet, red, smooth; bumpy, salty,
crunchy; gray, squeaky, furry

Page 21
Make-believe: ketchup bottles and a
watermelon bowling, a talking milk jug,
dancing bananas, chicken wings that
can fly all by themselves, laughing soup
cans, dancing carrots

Page 22
Answers will vary.

Page 23
A. 7 + 3 = 10; B. 7 – 4 = 3; C. 10 – 6 = 4;
D. 8 – 2 = 6; E. 5 + 4 = 9

Page 24
trash, flash, cash, sash, mash, rash,
splash, crash

```
s p x f h f r a s h x s n a g p p s h f
p s h f s n p s h f s p l a s h p s h f
c r a s h f s h n a g p p s h f c a s h
d p s r h w s a s h i r c m a s h i b v
s t a s h f g i s n a p t r a s h d s f
f g p f l a s h s n i a s m a s h b j k
```

Page 25
1. bear; 2. panda; 3. Jane; 4. dog;
5. wagon; 6. birds

Page 26
Answers will vary.

Page 27
6, 4, 2; 3, 1, 5
LEARN TO DIVE

Page 28
7 + 7 = 14; 5 + 5 = 10; 8 + 8 = 16;
6 + 6 = 12; 9 + 9 = 18; 3 + 3 = 6;
2 + 2 = 4; 4 + 4 = 8

Page 31
Check child's answers.

Page 32
Check child's answers.

Page 33
1. true; 2. false; 3. false; 4. true; 5. true

Page 34
Circle: What, See, Night; The, Light,
Moon; See, Many Stars; The, Sun, Moon;
Answers will vary.

Page 35
1. The pictures that do not belong are
bike, telephone, snowman, pumpkin,
skates, and frog. (The other pictures
should be colored.); 2. hot, cold; 3. up,
down; 4. starfish; 5. yellow

Page 36
Check child's work; red, white and blue;
stars and stripes; answers will vary;
answers will vary

Page 37
1. look, stars; 2. the, moon, shines, night;
3. we, see, planets; 4. many, moons,
shine; 5. night, day; 6. The Sun in the Sky;
7. See the Stars!

Page 38
sick, kick, chick, pick, lick, slick, thick, trick

```
e u y c k v c h b l k i c k t h c e k f
b j k t r i c k s p x f h q u i c k c k
u y v b l w i c k u y v b l c h i c k w
c k p i c k s p c h c k x f h s l i c k
t f h l i c k u c h y v b c k l s i c k
s p c c k h x f h t h i c k b c k j k h
```

Page 39
Answers will vary.

Page 40
Answers will vary.

Page 43

7 + 2 = 9 – 4 = 5 – 3 = 2 + 9 = 11 + 5 = 16 – 8 = 8 + 4 = 12 + 6 = 18 – 9 = 9 + 1 = 10 + 4 = 14 – 8 = 6 + 2 = 8 + 3 = 11 – 3 = 8; 12 – 3 = 9 – 6 = 3 + 2 = 5 + 9 = 14 – 6 = 8 + 7 = 15 – 6 = 9 + 3 = 12 – 2 = 10 + 7 = 17 + 1 = 18 – 11 = 7 – 5 = 2 + 13 = 15 – 7 = 8 + 3 = 11;
Color the bottom car blue.

Page 44

1. Where is the king's castle?
2. Who helped Humpty Dumpty?
3. Why did the cow jump over the moon?
4. Will the frog become a prince?
5. Could the three mice see?

Page 45

Check child's work.

Page 46

1. T, .
2. S, .
3. D, ?
4. I, ?
5. M, .
6. Will he take the cat home?

Page 47

Check child's work.

Page 48

1. E
2. C
3. E
4. E
5. E
6. C
7. Be yourself!
8. Don't copy other people.

Page 49

2, 4, 2; 3, 5, 4; 6, 4, 10; Answers will vary.

Page 50

1. T
2. C
3. T
4. C
5. Q
6. E
7. Q
8. I, Answers will vary.
9. I, Answers will vary.
10. I, Answers will vary.

Page 51

1. penguin; 2. baby; 3. octopus; 4. ant;
5. grandmother; 6. bear; 7. firefighter

Page 52

flight, knight, fight, slight, fright, might, light, tight

```
f l i g h t  s p c b j k h  m i g h t  f h
t s i h i d f d e b j s p h s d e t r i
u y b l  s i g h t  t h f  k n i g h t  h g
f i g h t  s p c b j k h x f h  t i g h t
t h f  r i g h t  u y v b c  l i g h t  h t
c  s l i g h t  h v h f s  r i g h t  u t y
```

Page 55

1. L; 2. D; 3. T; 4. W; 5. A; 6. B; 7. R; 8. E;
9. O; 10. S; 11. F; FAST FOOD; FLOWER BED

Page 56

Answers will vary.

Page 57

People, Places, and Things:
brother, school, children, sister
Action Words: ask, read, said, say, took
Describing Words: pretty, purple, funny, brown, short, white

Page 58

A. Sunday; B. 89; C. Monday; D. 24;
E. 79; F. 22; Sunday, Tuesday, Saturday

Page 61

Alex's coins: 25¢ + 25¢ + 10¢ = 60¢
Billy's coins: 10¢ + 10¢ + 10¢ + 10¢ +10¢ + 5¢ + 5¢ + 1¢ + 1¢ + 1¢ = 63¢
63¢ > 60¢. Billy has more money.

Page 62

bill, hill, drill, grill, will, quill, chill, sill

```
t c l h l h f  q u i l l  s p x f h t h f
c h i l l  u y l l b l  h i l l  t h f h l
c x f h  d r i l l  t h h f  g r i l l  s p
s i l l  s l p l f c l h h  b i l l  j k y
t l h f  w i l l  u c b v b l  t h r i l l
u l b l j k y v l c l h l b l  m i l l  u
```

Page 63

1. boy, boat
2. brothers, park
3. girl, grandmother
4. boats, lake
5. Friends, needle, thread, sail
People: boy, brothers, girl, grandmother, friends
Places: park, lake
Things: boat, boats, needle, thread, sail

Page 64

1. dogs and cats
2. Good Pets
3. run and jump

Page 67

1. dish
2. flower
3. clothing
4. dessert
5. animal
6. shape
7. tool
8. number

Page 68

1. children
2. car
3. clown
4. shoes
5. band
6. music
Answers will vary.

Page 69

Police officers help people.

Page 70

Answers will vary.

Page 71

Answers will vary. Check children's graphs to make sure that they correspond to the boxes checked. The following is a likely answer.
Chicken: see, hear, smell, touch
Sun: see
Lemonade: see, touch, taste
Flowers: see, smell, touch
Drums: see, hear, touch

Page 72

1. Sue
2. California
3. Los Angeles
4. Pacific Ocean
5. Tonya
6. Sue Wong
7. Shore Road
8. Austin, Texas
Answers will vary.

Scholastic Teaching Resources   *Get Ready for 2nd Grade*

Page 73

Page 74

sink, wink, drink, link, rink, think, stink, pink

s p x f h (t h i n k) t h f (s t i n k) y l
r e (p i n k) s p x f h (s i n k) t h c h f
t h f (w i n k) u y v b j k c h b n k i y
(d r i n k) s p b j k h (s h r i n k) t h f
u y v b j k b l (s l i n k) t h f (l i n k)
k b n k j k t h f (r i n k) s p x f n k h

Page 76

1/5 of the circle, 4/5 of the rectangle,
3 ants, 2 spiders, 0 bees, 5 worms

Page 80

gate, cane, game, rake, tray, snail, safe,
mane, cake, hay, cape, pail

Page 81

1. Jan has her mittens.
2. She will run up hills.
3. Jan runs with her dogs.
4. The dogs can jump.
5. cats
6. socks

Page 82

Make-believe: pig, goat and sheep,
pizza and hamburgers, mouse, crickets;
(The others are real.)

Page 83

1. girl
2. boys
3. dolls
4. lions
5. posters
6. balloons
7. balls
8. hoop
9. man
10. caps
11. shirts
12. hands
Answer will vary.

Page 84

Answers will vary.

Page 85

21, 93, 78, 46, 44, 78; PLEASE
50, 67, 46, 79, 83, 59, 25, 66; THANK YOU
59, 25, 66, 32, 78; YOU'RE
80, 78, 93, 18, 25, 35, 78; WELCOME

Page 86

rock, sock, smock, lock, flock, knock,
clock, dock

s p b j k x f h (r o c k) u c h y u v b l
(l o c k) u y c k v c k b l (f l o c k) i y
t h c k b j k h f (k n o c k) t h c k i f
(f r o c k) s p x b j k f h (s o c k) t h f
(c l o c k) t c h h c k f (d o c k) x f c k
t b j k h f (c r o c k) s p h (s m o c k) k

Answers will vary.

Page 87

3, 1, 4, 2, 6, 7, 5, 8

Page 88

Page 91

77 – 30 = 47; 76 – 62 = 14; 59 – 12 = 47
85 – 52 = 33; 98 – 84 = 14; 87 – 40 = 47
98 – 35 = 63; 58 – 11 = 47; 88 – 62 = 26
77 – 14 = 63; 69 – 22 = 47; 38 – 12 = 26
75 – 12 = 63; 97 – 71 = 26; 97 – 50 = 47
98 – 51 = 47; 43 – 10 = 33; 87 – 73 = 14
78 – 31 = 47; 97 – 64 = 33; 99 – 52 = 47

Page 92

1. kite
2. swing
3. vase
4. bat
5. wheel
6. bed
7. road
8. sock
9. cup

Page 95

People Who Went to the Beach: Dad,
Mom, Tim, Tara
What They Did: swam, fished, built
sandcastles, went sailing
Picnic Items: ham sandwiches, potato
chips, apples, cookies, lemonade
Living Things They Saw on the Beach:
crab, dog, starfish, seagulls

Page 96

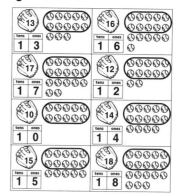

Page 97

1. He learned to fly.
2. All of a sudden something
wonderful happened.
3. afraid; 4. proud

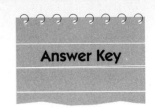

Page 98
1. runs
2. wears
3. smacks
4. holds
5. misses
6. waits
7. writes
8. helps
Answers will vary.

Page 99
1. watch
2. throws
3. opens
4. cheers
5. hits
6. runs
7. yells
8. eat

Page 100
bump, grump, jump, stump, hump, pump, plump, dump

u y c h v b l s t u m p s p x p l u m p
f h u m p u c h y v f h b l j u m p p m
o p g m h b u m p mp c h g r u m p s t
j s d b n h k m p p u m p s p m p x f h
d u m p t h c h f c l u m p w s p x f h
t c m p e r c a b t h j k h h f l u m p

Page 103
A. 52, 93, 72, 93; B. 41, 62, 37, 37;
C. 23, 50, 62, 62; D. 60, 32, 81, 60;
E. 90, 44, 76, 44

Page 104
1. planted
2. watered
3. weeded
4. discovered
5. (blank)
6. pulled

Page 105
1. pushed
2. splashed
3. rolled
4. followed
5. washed

Page 106
Check child's work.

Page 107
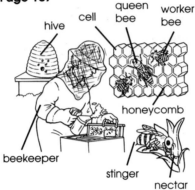

hive — cell — queen bee — worker bee — honeycomb — beekeeper — stinger — nectar

Page 108
trunk, chunk, skunk, hunk, bunk, shrunk, sunk, stunk
Answers will vary.

m n s k u n k s p x h h u n k s p x f h
h k v b l t r u n k k m n u y i c n b h
k n k m s u n k s p x f h b u n k k m n
u y c h b l s t u n k s p k x f h n j k
k j u n k t h f d u n k k m p x n k m n
m n c h u n k u y c h l c h s h r u n k

Page 109
A. 48, 89; 48
B. 79, 46; 46
C. 36, 76; 76
D. 77, 59; 77
E. 48, 14; 48
F. 61, 68; 68
G. 14, 39; 39
Answers will vary.

Page 110
Sentences will vary.

Page 111
1. spewing hot lava and ash into the air;
2. for people and animals to breathe;
3. flattened trees; 4. forest fires; 5. floods and mudslides; 6. it still erupts from time to time

Page 112
Answers will vary.

Page 115
Check child's work.

Page 116
1. groups of whales
2. Whales
3. stay wet
4. to get air

Page 117
1. noun
2. verb
3. noun
4. verb
5. verb
6. noun
7. verb
8. noun
9. noun
10. verb
Answers will vary.

Page 118
1. 5
2. 8
3. 11
4. 26
5. 6
6. 10
7. 12
8. 16
9. 18
10. 24
What did the rocket say when it left the party? "Time to take off."

Page 119
2. X
3. X
6. Dr. Smileyface makes his patients laugh. 7. The child who wrote this story is not afraid to go to the dentist. 8. Dr. Smileyface teaches kids how to take care of their teeth. 9. Dr. Smileyface sends kids home with a surprise.

Page 120
Who: sister, children, men, us
Where: here, school, there
When: after, before, now, soon

Page 121
1/7 of the candy; 4/7 of the candy; no, the bread only has 7 slices; 7 bananas; 3 jars

Page 123
75, 62, 81, 50, 44, 60;
95, 97, 45, 58, 85, 91

Page 124
Answers will vary.

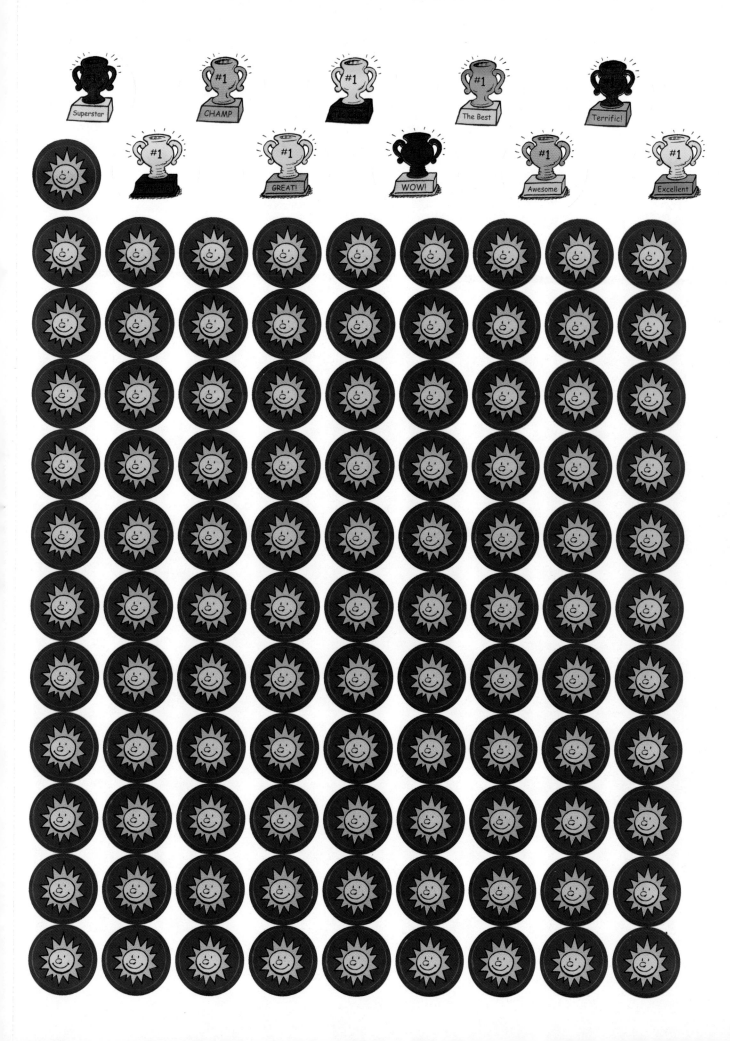